Practicing Social Justice in Libraries

Practicing Social Justice in Libraries provides practical strategies, tools, and resources to library and information workers and students who wish to drive change in their classrooms, institutions, and communities and incorporate social justice into their everyday practice.

With contributions from a diverse group of librarians, who have experience working in different types of institutions and roles, the book showcases the actions information professionals, largely from historically marginalized groups, are taking to create a more socially responsible environment for themselves and their communities. The chapters reflect on personal experiences, best practices for programming, professional development, effective collaboration, building inclusive community partnerships, anti-racist practices in the classroom, and organizational culture. Exploring how and why library workers are incorporating anti-racist and anti-oppressive work within their everyday roles, the book demonstrates that library workers are increasingly sending messages of protest and advocating for equity, justice, and social change. Highlighting their experiences of marginalization and exclusion, contributors also reflect upon the impact social justice work has on their mental health, careers, and personal lives.

Practicing Social Justice in Libraries is essential reading for library and information workers and students who are searching for practical ways to implement more inclusive practices into their work.

Alyssa Brissett is an academic librarian. Her research interests include critical library practice, organizational change and culture, and social justice in libraries. She graduated with her MLIS from Wayne State University and has a Master of Arts in childhood education from New York University.

Diana Moronta is an academic librarian. Her research interests include critical library instruction, open educational resources, and social justice in libraries. She graduated with her MSLIS from Pratt Institute and her BA from Hunter College, City University of New York.

Routledge Guides to Practice in Libraries, Archives and Information Science

This series provides essential practical guides for those working in libraries, archives, and a variety of other information science professions around the globe.

Including authored and edited volumes, the series will help to enhance practitioners' and students' professional knowledge and will also encourage sharing of best practices between different countries, as well as between different types and sizes of organisations.

Guidance for Librarians Transitioning to a New Environment
Tina Herman Buck and Sara Duff

Recordkeeping in International Organizations
Archives in Transition in Digital, Networked Environments
Edited by Jens Boel and Eng Sengsavang

Trust and Records in an Open Digital Environment
Edited by Hrvoje Stančić

Assessment as Information Practice
Evaluating Collections and Services
Edited by Gaby Haddow and Hollie White

A Guide to Using the Anonymous Web in Libraries and Information Organizations
Enhancing Patron Privacy and Information Access
Brady D. Lund and Matthew A. Beckstrom

Practicing Social Justice in Libraries
Edited by Alyssa Brissett and Diana Moronta

For more information about this series, please visit: https://www.routledge.com/Routledge-Guides-to-Practice-in-Libraries-Archives-and-Information-Science/book-series/RGPLAIS

Practicing Social Justice in Libraries

Edited by
Alyssa Brissett
and Diana Moronta

Routledge
Taylor & Francis Group

LONDON AND NEW YORK

Cover image: Nayanba Jadeja / Getty Images

First published 2023
by Routledge
4 Park Square, Milton Park, Abingdon, Oxon OX14 4RN

and by Routledge
605 Third Avenue, New York, NY 10158

Routledge is an imprint of the Taylor & Francis Group,
an informa business

British Library Cataloguing-in-Publication Data
A catalogue record for this book is available from the British Library

Library of Congress Cataloging-in-Publication Data
A catalog record has been requested for this book

ISBN: 978-0-367-76491-3 (hbk)
ISBN: 978-0-367-76490-6 (pbk)
ISBN: 978-1-003-16717-4 (ebk)

DOI: 10.4324/9781003167174

Typeset in Times New Roman
by KnowledgeWorks Global Ltd.

For people who lift as they climb

Contents

Illustrations

Figures

Table

Contributors

Stefani Baldivia is an Archivist at CSU Chico, where she engages in reference, instruction, and outreach activities to promote the Special Collections. Her research interests include Latinx leadership in libraries, anti-colonial approaches to archival work, teaching with primary sources, and diversifying collections through oral histories.

Anthony Bishop is an Assistant Professor/Instructional Design Librarian with The Borough of Manhattan Community College (BMCC) in New York City. Previous publications include Diao, J., Tzanova, S., and Bishop, A. D. (2021). "Wikipedia and Scholarpedia: A comparative case study and its implications to information literacy." *Codex: The Journal of the Louisiana Chapter of the ACRL.* And Bishop A.D & Moffat, K. (2016). "Experiencing whiteness of LIS education: an autoethnography account". In Cura, Y. S., & Macias, M. (2016) Librarians with Spines: Information Agitators in an Age of Stagnation by HINCHAS Press.

Nataly Blas is a Latinx Librarian, first-generation student, and coffee enthusiast. She is interested in mentorship (both students and early career librarians), issues of equity and access in libraries, and women in leadership. Nataly can be found hiking, Bollywood dancing, or trying a new LA restaurant.

Peggy Cabrera is an Associate Librarian at San Josè State University. Cabrera's personal and academic interests focus on learning how we can develop deeper relationships with each other and with our environment. She enjoys sharing search strategies with students and seeing their growth as researchers. She also really enjoys planting seeds, growing food, and finding new recipes.

Elizabeth A. Carroll is a Faculty in the Department of Art and Art History (SJSU, USA) and leads a Faculty-Led Program in Venice, Italy. She is co-editor of *A Cultural History of Furniture in the Age of Exploration* Volume 3: (1500–1700), published in Fall 2021 by Bloomsbury Academic.

Atmaza Chattopadhyay is an international student from Singapore who is pursuing her undergraduate degree in the Bachelor of Arts at UBC Okanagan. She is an International Baccalaureate Diploma holder and has now settled in Kelowna, British Columbia, to pursue her tertiary education.

Aisha Conner-Gaten, she/her/hers, is an Information Worker thriving in Los Angeles. She is an organizer of the POC in LIS Summit and Librarians of Color-Los Angeles group, along with her incredible colleagues. Her work focuses on inclusive instructional design, antiracism in the library and pedagogy, and the role of librarians as social justice accomplices. When she is not at the reference desk, you can find her reading romance or playing tennis. You can follow her and her library quips on Twitter @Aisha_CG.

Karleen Delaurier-Lyle is Anishinabek, Cree, and of mixed settler ancestry. She is an enrolled member of Berens River First Nation, born and raised on the unceded, ancestral, and traditional Syilx/Okanagan territory. She is the Information Services Librarian for the X̱wi7x̱wa Library.

Joy Marie Doan (M.L.I.S., M.A.) is an Assistant Professor of Practice in the School of Information Sciences at the University of Tennessee, Knoxville. Professor Doan has (co)authored articles that center on academic library outreach to various student groups (i.e., international students and graduate students), as well as diversity in libraries.

Sarah Dupont, Métis, is the Head Librarian of the X̱wi7x̱wa Library at the University of British Columbia (UBC), on unceded xʷməθkʷəy̓əm (Musqueam) Territory in Vancouver, B.C., Canada. Ms. Dupont is one author of the article *Indigenization of Knowledge Organization at the X̱wi7x̱wa Library* (https://dx.doi.org/10.14288/1.0103204).

Jina DuVernay is the Program Director for Engagement and African American Collections at the Atlanta University Center's Robert W. Woodruff Library. She is the author of a chapter titled "Making Connections Between Archival Collections and Current Events" in the upcoming edited volume, Critical Ethnic Studies in Academic and Research Libraries.

Rebecca Hankins is the Wendler Endowed Professor and certified archivist/librarian. She is an affiliated faculty in Africana Studies, Women's & Gender Studies, and Religious Studies, where she also serves as subject liaison. She has published widely on diverse topics related to race, gender, and social justice.

Chrissy Hursh is a Resource Sharing Assistant for the University of Oregon in Eugene, OR, United States. Her other publications include "Teaching students how to read and critically evaluate scholarly articles in the sciences and agriculture" and "Teaching the kitchen sink: Active learning and peer teaching."

Taya Jardine is a Mi'gmaw woman from Natoaganeg First Nation, she holds a Bachelor's Degree in Cultural Studies with a minor in Indigenous Studies and is currently pursuing her Master of Library and Information Studies at the UBC School of Information.

Rahni B. Kennedy is the Music and Media Catalog/Metadata Librarian and Physical Processing Manager at Southern Methodist University. He currently serves as chair of the Texas Chapter of the Music Library Association (MLA) and as a member of the Encoding Standards Subcommittee of the MLA Cataloging and Metadata Committee. He holds a Doctor in Musical Arts degree in Clarinet Performance from Texas Tech University and an MSLS from the University of North Texas.

Sajni Lacey is a settler woman living in Kelowna, British Columbia, in what is now called Canada. She is the Learning and Curriculum Support Librarian at the University of British Columbia Okanagan Library.

Kayla Lar-Son is Metis and Ukrainian settler ancestry, originally from Treaty Six territory, Tofield, Alberta. She currently resides in the unceded territories of the $x^w m \partial \theta k^w \partial \dot{y} \partial m$ (Musqueam), S̲k̲wx̱wú7mesh (Squamish), and Selil̓witulh (Tsleil-Waututh) Nations in what is now known as Vancouver, BC. At UBC, Kayla is the Indigenous programs and services librarian at the X̱wi7xwa Library and is the program manager librarian for the Indigitization program.

Jennifer Masunaga (she/her/hers) is an Instruction and Reference Librarian at California State University, Los Angeles. Jennifer is a Mexicanese (Mexican American and Japanese American) Los Angeles native, and her research interests include diversity in librarianship, Library UX, IL Assessment, and fake news and misinformation. She also enjoys disaster preparedness and raising her daughter since both use the same skillset.

Essraa Nawar has been the Development Librarian and the Chair of the Arts, Exhibits and Events Committee at the Leathery Libraries at Chapman University, California, since 2009, where she helped raise over 5 million dollars in support of the Libraries and leads the Diversity, Equity and Inclusion Initiatives.

Kristine Nowak is a Librarian and Assistant Professor at Colorado State University in Fort Collins, Colorado, United States. She focuses on first-year instruction and diversity, equity, and inclusion in the library space. She received her MLIS from the University of Kentucky in 2011.

Stephanie Porrata is a Mary P. Key Diversity Resident Librarian for Area Studies at the Ohio State University in Columbus, Ohio, United States.

Zohra Saulat is a Student Success Librarian for Lake Forest College in Lake Forest, IL, United States. Her other publications include "Let's Take a Moment: Student Reflections and Reframing Research as a Journey" and

"God is a Woman: Finding Inspiration to Teach Information Literacy through Popular Music Videos."

Khaleedah Thomas is an Assistant Professor and Copyright Scholarly Communication Librarian at Colorado State University in Fort Collins, Colorado, United States. She holds an M.L.I.S. in Library and Information Science and an M.S. in Justice Studies from San Jose State University.

Shaunda Vasudev is the Outreach & Engagement Librarian at Capital University. She received her MLS from North Carolina Central University. Shaunda has also worked as a Youth Librarian in Columbus, OH, and Portland, OR, and in public, school, and special libraries in Charlotte, NC.

Renae J. Watson is an Assistant Professor and Librarian at Colorado State University in Fort Collins, Colorado, United States. She holds an M.S.Ed. in Learning Design and Technology, an M.S.L.S. in Library and Information Science, and an M.A. in English.

Jessea Young is an Oral Historian and Digital Collections Librarian. She is interested in tattoos as identity, issues of gentrification and settler colonialism within the Asian American community, and the history of Yellow Peril. Jessea can be found eating ice cream or huaraches with her dachshund terrier, Neville.

Acknowledgments

We are two librarians and friends who worked on this book across the country, one in Los Angeles and the other one in New York. We acknowledge that we live and work on the unceded lands of the Lenni-Lenape Peoples of New York and the Tongva (Gabrielino) People(Native Land Digital) As we dive into the ways that our communities create programs, policies, and exhibits around social justice issues, we are aware that libraries do not exist in a vacuum and are institutions built on systemic oppression and perpetuate and produce hostile and violent environments against Indigenous people, Black people, People of Color, and other historically marginalized communities.

A heartfelt thank you to the contributors for their creativity, generosity, and the passion they brought to their work and for bringing that same passion to the communities they serve. We wouldn't have a book without you.

We acknowledge each other for the labor and love we put into this project while navigating a pandemic, the increasing social injustices in the United States, our personal lives, and stressful work environments. We learned a lot about ourselves, our profession, and our friendship was strengthened throughout this project. We supported, encouraged, and mentored each other through the difficult parts of the process. We learned conflict resolution within a friendship, and we grew from this experience.

Lastly, our love and gratitude to our moms Oneida and Elara, and a special thank you to Diego, LeeAnn, Jasmin, Stacy, our friends, our families, our mentors, and our communities. We are grateful for your continued encouragement, feedback, guidance, kindness, and the ways you sustain us and help us thrive.

Reference

Native Land Digital, Territory Acknowledgment. https://native-land.ca/resources/territory-acknowledgement/

Introduction

Alyssa Brissett and Diana Moronta

Introduction

As friends and colleagues, we have always served as each other's sounding board, starting our careers as librarians around the same time in 2017. Although we were living and working in different states, we experienced a lot of the same "firsts" and had many of the same ideas and thoughts about library work. This book was an enlightening experience for us, where we learned a lot about ourselves, what we are capable of, our profession, and where we see ourselves and our work in this profession. Collaborating remotely across the country and co-editing while living and working during a pandemic added an unusual strain to our work, but one that we're happy to see come to fruition.

When we set out to do the work that would ultimately materialize in the book you are about to read, we intended to build on our previous work and research around how librarians use LibGuides as a response to the social injustices in the United States and advocate for themselves and their communities. Initially, the goal of our research was to examine the recent increase in diversity, equity, and inclusion initiatives in librarianship.

Some questions we had very early on in our collaboration were, "what does diversity really mean?", "what does "diversity work" look like in librarianship?" "how are librarians implementing social justice elements into their daily work as instructors, directors, catalogers, and in the many other titles librarians hold within libraries?" and "how are librarians protesting and resisting in their everyday work?". We questioned the authenticity of the anti-racism and anti-oppression sentiments that became a trend in the Library and Information Science (LIS) field.

In 2018, we continued our research and gathered preliminary data through a survey to identify and reflect on the work that librarians and other information professionals do around social justice and equity and its impact on their communities, their work, and themselves. Using feedback from that initial survey, we expanded to include questions that gathered data around mental health for Black, Indigenous, and People of Color (BIPOC) librarians doing anti-racist/anti-colonialist/anti-oppression work.

DOI: 10.4324/9781003167174-1

This revised action plan allowed us to strategize about where to send the survey and expand our variables to include not only libguides but any area where library and information workers find themselves doing anti-racist work. We wanted to highlight how library and information workers practice social justice in their everyday work, including creating libguides, events, exhibits, and programming and sharing practical resources and examples. We saw our colleagues doing this work and wanted to highlight the important resources that went into creating safer, more accessible, and equitable spaces for ourselves and our communities.

Our book demonstrates how information workers implement inclusive practices in and around our work across institutions, communities, and collaborations in the field of librarianship. Our plan was to add to the scholarship of library and information science concerned with social justice and building more equitable and inclusive spaces. We explore and examine how librarians and other information professionals use these tools and resources to drive change in their classrooms, institutions, and communities. Through everyday practice, including instruction, reference, collection development, and interactions with their communities, librarians are sending messages of protest and advocating for equity, political and social change.

It is a collection of experiences, resources, and guidelines for information workers from various library settings, and backgrounds who have shared how they have resisted, created programs, advocated, practiced, and addressed issues within their workplaces to foster more open, just, and inclusive spaces.

It is for library workers who are frustrated with the lack of practical applications, the talk about increasing diversity without concrete actions, and those who are searching for practical ways to implement more inclusive practices into their work. This is an opportunity for us to highlight some voices that are doing this work in libraries and share our own passion for creating more just and safe spaces for ourselves and our patrons.

Our collection starts out with a chapter from three Black librarians, **Anthony Bishop, Jina DuVernay, and Rebecca Hankins,** who provide an account of their experiences at their individual libraries shortly after the murder of George Floyd in 2020 and the uprisings that fueled resistances and movements across the country. In Chapter 2, four colleagues, **Jennifer Masunaga, Aisha Conner-Gaten, Nataly Blas, and Jessea Young,** discuss creating safe spaces for BIPOC library workers, establishing a LIS conference intended to empower voices and build community. In Chapter 3, the essay by **Shaunda Vasudev** highlights a collaboration with campus partners, including student organizations, to improve social justice through outreach and programming on a college campus.

The essay by **Stephanie Porrata** in Chapter 4 discusses the opportunities and limitations of libguides as a social justice tool. Authors **Sarah Dupont, Karleen Delaurier-Lyle, and Kayla Lar-Son,** in Chapter 5, highlight Indigenous librarianship and how libguides allow them to share lived experiences and realities through an Indigenous and social justice lens.

The book continues with Chapter 6, with author **Essraa Nawar** and her clear examples of how to create, organize, and market library events, exhibits, and displays centered on ethnically and gender-diverse collections. Chapter 7 focuses on the collaboration between librarian, **Peggy Cabrera,** and lecturer **Elizabeth A. Carroll**. Their semester-long interaction brings to focus socially responsible building design to increase awareness of sustainability (equity, economics, and environment). In this chapter, they describe the foundation of their partnership and strategies they brought to the classroom to maintain student engagement through online learning due to covid-19.

Chapter 8 continues with **Renae J. Watson, Khaleedah Thomas, and Kristine Nowak** and their experience forming an ad-hoc group to automate the ordering of diverse books, integrating inclusive collections into their daily work, and advocating for an equitable, anti-racist collection. The authors leave the readers with practical strategies and advice for librarians on how to create equitable and inclusive collections in their libraries.

Chapter 9 focuses on the creation of an equity, inclusion, and diversity internship program at the University of British Columbia Okanagan Library by **Sajni Lacey, Taya Jardine, and Atmaza Chattopadhyay** and the personal reflections from the perspective of the hiring librarian and the two interns hired for the position, as well as, how this position was created and structured. Chapter 10 centers on how librarians **Stefani Baldivia, Zohra Saulat,** and **Chrissy Hursh** implemented strategies from adrienne maree brown's Emergent Strategy: Shaping Change, Changing Worlds for the library self-care community. And Chapter 11, the last chapter of this collection by **Joy Doan and Rahni B. Kennedy**, focuses on diversity fatigue, where the authors look at the systemic structure of diversity work in libraries and how it affects BIPOC library workers.

We hope that you find this collection useful and it inspires you to implement these strategies, policies, and programming at your own libraries to further continue your commitment and activism for social justice while working in libraries.

1 Black Librarianship in the Times of Racial Unrest

An Ethnographic Study from Three Black Voices

Anthony Bishop, Jina DuVernay,
and Rebecca Hankins

Introduction

Public lynchings were common throughout the 18th and 19th centuries in the United States. They were advertised and crowds of people attended them. Souvenirs, photographs, and postcards of the lynched were shared all over the country. Ida B. Wells crusaded around the country for anti-lynching laws to be enacted at the Federal level but found very little support, and to this date, the bill has not passed. In 2018, the Senate passed anti-lynching legislation, but the House had not approved it; however, in 2020, in response to the murder of Floyd, the House passed the bill. When it was returned to the Senate for approval, Senator Rand Paul held it up and the bill currently sits in limbo (Fandos, 2020). With this as a backdrop, the date of May 26, 2020, in Minneapolis, Minnesota, will always be a day of infamy in American history. The world witnessed a slow "lynching" of a Black man, George Floyd, which was captured on video. What we saw with the public *lynching* of Floyd is representative of the dismissal of these incidents with the *souvenir* of our time, video evidence shared all over the country and world.

As people around the world viewed the unconscionable murder of George Floyd, many library administrators and white colleagues looked to their Black library staff to respond to the social climate of 2020. This chapter will relay how each library where we work, Texas A&M University (TAMU), College Station (Texas-Rebecca Hankins), Emory University, Atlanta (Georgia-Jina DuVernay), and Borough of Manhattan Community College (BMCC), New York (New York-Anthony Bishop), responded to the historic events of 2020 and their efforts to reckon with the history of systemic racism in America. We are all at predominantly white institutions (PWI), while the overall geographic environments were different, two in the South (TAMU and Emory) and one in the North. Emory is situated in Atlanta, a predominantly Black liberal city, while TAMU is in a more rural and very conservative environment. BMCC is located in a large, diverse, and liberal urban city. The southern universities are also very different, one more rural and conservative (TAMU) and the other (Emory) in a predominantly African American

DOI: 10.4324/9781003167174-2

and liberal city. Additionally, we will share how we, as Black archivists and librarians, aided in the efforts of each library while advancing our own interests by advocating for social justice through programming, outreach, education, and collection building. Our ethnographic approach to the chapter seeks to ground our work in our individual experiences, giving insight into our perspectives about each library's reaction to the social climate.

Texas A&M University

TAMU has a history like many other southern land-grant institutions. Many of these academic institutions were founded to educate all citizens, but quickly enacted laws to segregate them. Most of these laws followed the 14th Amendment when formerly freed slaves were given full citizenship. For example, after its founding in 1876, TAMU quickly declared, "it is an unalterable principle engrafted on the constitution and laws to prevent an admixture of the white and colored races in the common and higher schools of learning ... that no applicant for admission as a student shall be received unless of the white race" (The Independent, 1877).

The George Floyd murder, along with the rage so many people felt, was exacerbated by learning of the killing of Ahmaud Arbery and Breonna Taylor. All the pent-up fears and anger boiled over, and people took to the streets. On June 1st, the TAMU University President sent out an email of condolences while also claiming Floyd as an alumnus because he attended Texas A&M Kingsville. The email spoke of systemic racism but not the university's part in the system. The email did not mention that Floyd was murdered by a police officer or mention the Black Lives Matter Movement that has stood up for racial justice. The email was mostly about how "the university's core values of *Honor, Integrity, Respect, and Selfless Service* are exemplified" (Core Values, 2021) without saying how those values were unconnected to what the world witnessed on the day of Floyd's murder. The President's message was discussed with the library's Diversity Advancement Committee (DAC), where membership is open to the entire library and members spoke of these inadequacies. The conversation that ensued over email was important in allowing the committee to discuss what actions, activities, or possible work we could do to counter the stressful feelings that many were experiencing.

The dean of the libraries at TAMU, a white male, also engaged the library to discuss the President's letter, where he was pushed to understand that it was not only that A&M's history of white supremacy and racism was unacknowledged, but on campus, there is the statue of Lawrence Sullivan Ross, a Confederate General, that is upheld as a symbol of respect. Many of us tied that disconnect from the President's email on racism and hatred to this dichotomy of white supremacy on continuous display. These exchanges prompted the Latino Studies and Africana Studies departments, where I am an affiliate faculty member and library subject liaison, to write a joint letter of support for an honest telling of A&M's history and the removal of the Ross statue. To this day, our concerns have gone unheeded.

The library at TAMU has a population of over 89 full-time faculty, approximately 11 Black, Indigenous, People of Color (BIPOC) members. I am the only tenured African American Full Professor in the library and have been for over ten years. There is one other African American faculty member who is a Lecturer. When I arrived at the library in 2003, there were at least seven African American faculty members, but we have lost all of these formerly tenure track and tenured librarians. The archival field and Cushing Memorial Library & Archives, where most of my work is centered, have even fewer African Americans than in the librarian field. In my 18+ years at Cushing, there have only been three other People of Color in faculty or staff positions, the last person leaving in 2008. Despite those statistics, the dean has been extremely supportive of diversity efforts, funding programs, collections, and other initiatives with a diversity, equity, and inclusion (DEI) focus. More importantly, the dean has chosen to speak up and put in writing thoughts on these troubled times when no one at the university level will. It was under his leadership that the DAC changed its name to include Advancement to be more proactive rather than reactive.

Our DAC, where I am a member, also ramped up its social justice work that had already seen the hiring of DeEtta Jones and Associates to begin year-long strategic planning that sought to make concrete changes in the library by integrating DEI throughout our practices and processes (Jones, 2020). The librarians also created more library guides related to anti-racism and social justice that included statements, videos, books for children, and other resources available within the library. I included an essay on Juneteenth that chronicles the history of enslaved people in Texas. These efforts continue to be acknowledged by others on campus and throughout the country, where we have received requests to add our work to other guides and workshops. These were mostly passive means of activism, but we looked for more active ways to engage in social justice that would be much more constructive and forceful in educating the public, especially on campus.

I decided to take on the mythology of Lawrence Sullivan Ross using archival and library resources to discuss the history and implications of the Confederacy to not just his service to uphold slavery, but also his massacre of Indigenous Native Americans, Mexicans, and Black Union soldiers. If you are decrying violence and injustice, then how do you reconcile that with having a Confederate statue on campus. The students and faculty took up this mantle, too, protesting and writing about the history of Ross and the plea to remove it from campus. The University created a 45-person commission of students, former students, faculty, and staff to evaluate DEI to discuss these issues, but notably, no current member from the library or Cushing, where TAMU's history and materials are housed, was included except for the retired director of Cushing (Membership, 2020). The omission of current library representation on the commission was strange in that there were three acting university archivists available during this period. The results of the commission did not include the removal of the Sul Ross statue, nor was it addressed in the final report (Report, 2021).

This movement to uncover the slave-holding and racist heritage of our academic institutions in the United States was highlighted during Brown University's President Ruth Simmons's tenure, where she offered an apology for that history. Through the prism of these demonstrations and activism after the death of George Floyd, many universities saw the need to also investigate and work toward making amends for their controversial histories. This led me to create a presentation titled *Capturing Controversy & Digitizing Racism: Yearbooks at Texas A&M University 1895–2014* (Hankins, 2021. Central to this presentation was centering Lawrence Sullivan Ross and his life as a Confederate General that I soon discovered was not what most people wanted to hear about or focus on. Despite this desire to obscure or deflect from the university's upholding of this Confederate General's statue, this presentation has done more to further the discussions on campus on race, social justice, institutional heritage, and difficult dialogues regarding statues and monuments than any of my other work.

The most significant of those activities is the History Department's Summer Undergraduate Research Experience course titled *Black Lives Matter at Texas A&M, Texas, and the World,* where I and a colleague worked closely with the professor on resources and activities. We created a library guide (Hankins, 2021) for the course, pulling together the library and archival resources that students used to develop anti-racism projects to either publish, perform, or create some product that will provide a lasting memory to pass on to others. During this six-week program, I provided Zoom presentations on three separate occasions and met with individual students for one-on-one consultations to assist them with their subjects. I helped them to refine, focus, and develop their projects with relevant resources.

For one of the class meetings, I shared archivist Caitlin Rivas Sullivan's article titled "Understanding the Archivist's Role in Contextualization, Removal, and Relocation of Confederate Monuments at Cultural Heritage Institutions" (Rivas Sullivan, 2019), which discussed monuments from the perspective of archivists. The professor had the class read the article, and we discussed it after I provided a PowerPoint presentation on monuments and statues that discussed their history, both positive and negative, and the current removal of Confederate statues that are occurring around the country. I sought to contextualize these discussions and how this relates to A&M's Confederate statue that has been the center of protests, debates, and controversy.

The students at TAMU have continued to protest throughout the Summer and Fall semesters. I have been invited to speak repeatedly to several student groups, individually, organizations, and via academic classes on monuments and statues. The library has strongly supported these efforts that we see as an important part of our commitment to educate, inform, and to be, as our motto states, "an indispensable hub of discovery, learning, and creativity." As you read my colleagues' stories below, you will see similarities and differences that we will sum up in the Conclusion.

Emory Libraries

Emory University is a PWI located in Atlanta, Georgia's most populous city. The city, with its rich history related to the Civil Rights Movement, is predominantly Black making up 51% of the population. These demographics were not lost on Yolanda Cooper, Dean and University Librarian of Emory Libraries. She, like many of her staff, sought out ways to respond to the historic social climate of summer 2020 that resulted from that fateful day, May 26th, that George Floyd was casually murdered in broad daylight in the middle of a Minneapolis, Minnesota, street by a police officer.

One of the ways that Dean Cooper acted in response to the social climate was by commissioning a series of blog posts that would address the influx of requests from students for information around racial injustice. More specifically, many students were looking for archival material related to past Black student demands as they were in the process of drafting their own 2020 student demands. Dean Cooper identified three members of her staff, one of which was me, from different departments and areas of expertise to highlight archival and library resources. She wanted us to write narratives about the relevance of the resources to the current events such as protests, the disenfranchisement of Black voters, and most notably, the horrific murder of Breonna Taylor, George Floyd, and countless other Black citizens at the hands of police and white vigilantes. As a result, I, along with my two other colleagues, researched, organized, and wrote four blog posts collectively called Racial Blog Series (Bruchko, et al, 2020) We published one blog post each month during the fall semester and provided students, faculty, and the Emory community with the helpful resources that were available to them. Blog topics included Black student activism at Emory, protests, and movements, voting rights and public policy, and authors and artists as activists.

As a Black woman herself, Dean Cooper, understood the toll that relentless racial violence against Black people can take on them. The recognition of the potential effects of Black people being murdered in their own homes or in broad daylight in the street might have on her Black staff prompted the concerned and proactive dean to create space for them to gather and support one another during the tumultuous time. Allowing the Black members of her staff to convene for an hour on an ongoing basis as often as they needed was yet another way that Dean Cooper responded to the social climate of spring and summer of 2020.

She asked her administrative assistant to invite the Black library staff members to a meeting that was held via Zoom. Additionally, Dean Cooper asked her assistant and me to co-facilitate the group meetings. During the initial meeting, Dean Cooper spoke to her Black staff and informed them that she wanted them to feel supported and valued in the libraries. She let the staff know that they were welcome to continue to meet after the initial meeting to express themselves among other Black people if they so wished.

I was honored to have been asked to help facilitate the group of my Black colleagues, many of whom I had not met before since we were all at different Emory libraries. As a member of the Emory Libraries DEI Professional Development subcommittee, I felt prepared for the task. I had been working with the DEI subcommittee to create productive programming for our colleagues in the library to promote healthy and necessary discussions about systemic racism. Very few Black colleagues attended these programs, so I looked forward to being with and supporting the group.

The group continued to meet after the first meeting. Many discussed the trauma that they experience when they see people that look like their own relative or friend being murdered on a constant basis. They talked about how triggering videos on social media can be as well as the non-stop television coverage of the tragic deaths of Black people. Moreover, the group shared the microaggressions that they encounter in the workplace. After hearing what some of the staff said, my co-facilitator and I decided to invite a Black human resources representative to the group to answer any questions about the most effective way to report inappropriate incidents. At other meetings, we invited the chair of the Emory Libraries DEI committee, as well as Emory University's Chief Diversity Officer. The Black library staff continued to have informal meetings via Zoom after the meetings that included invited guests. These meetings began to serve as a reprieve from feelings of isolation, being disrespected, or devalued that some experienced in the workplace. Conversations began to turn to pop culture, book discussions, professional development opportunities, and mostly about politics.

Other library initiatives that were being talked about prior to the murder of George Floyd began to take shape, transforming discussions of various important projects to actual implementation. One such initiative was that of drafting a code of conduct for the library personnel. While the idea is basic enough, it did not get traction until Dean Cooper listened to what some of the Black library staff shared in that initial meeting. It was determined that the present was the opportune time to create a code of conduct. Representatives from groups and teams around the library were asked to volunteer to serve on the code of conduct task force.

Another initiative that had long been contemplated and discussed was the need to remediate harmful language that can be found in the finding aids. During the summer of 2020, the efforts of the small team of archivists, including myself, who work at the Stuart A. Rose Manuscript, Archives, and Rare Book Library, ramped up. We began meeting more often to work on a statement about potential harmful language that would display on every finding aid. We also began to work on guidelines for Rose Library archivists to eliminate harmful language when possible when writing finding aids.

Catalogers in the Woodruff Library also started to work more aggressively at remediating entries in the catalog. Library and archives professionals worked diligently to make positive, overdue changes as they thought critically about how systemic racism is manifested within librarianship. All in all, there was and continues to be active participation in the abovementioned initiatives, which all receive full support from Dean Cooper. Under her leadership, her staff has been empowered to create, organize, and participate in initiatives that prioritize DEI in a myriad of ways. The work that we were able to put our energy and passion into in 2020 served as a vital outlet for many, a way to affect changes in uncertain times.

Borough of Manhattan Community College

As I woke up the morning of May 26, 2020, a cloud of confusion hung over me. The day before, I witnessed George Floyd calling out for his mother as he took his last breath of life under the knee of Minneapolis police officer Derrick Chauvin, and it left me wounded on many levels as an African American male who has witnessed similar atrocities play out between police officers and Black men in the United States for decades. As I prepared for my virtual workday at the BMCC, I anticipated that white people everywhere would feel compelled to express their sympathy to all African Americans that day. Since my department was working virtually, I felt the lack of person-to-person communication would make it easier for my white colleagues to express their feelings to the People of Color in our department via email or text. I expected to be flooded with emails and text messages discussing the incident of the day before, but to my surprise, I was met with eerie silence. One day passed, then another, but although my department was silent on this tragedy, the world was not. In the days that followed, protests took place all over the country and Minneapolis became "ground zero" for a racial justice movement.

As the workweek ended, I entered the weekend observing mass protests not only across America but across the globe. When I returned to work virtually that following Monday, a week after the tragedy, I could no longer keep quiet, so I started my workday that morning by drafting an email expressing my frustration as a Black man in America witnessing the events of the previous week. The demographic makeup of our library department at BMCC is diverse, including librarians of color (Asian Pacific Islander, Latinx, and African Americans). In my lengthy email, I expressed the pain that the repetition of witnessing systemic racism against African American men had taken on me, not only as a Black man but also as a Black librarian who too often had to suffer in silence on the job when events like this took place because of my minority status in the department. Taking a pause, I reviewed my email, pondered the results of it throughout the department, and I clicked send.

I waited in anticipation for the responses my email would garner. To my pleasant surprise, I received immediate and overwhelmingly supportive responses. It was as if my department was waiting for me, as one of the two only Black librarians in the department, to jumpstart the conversation within the department that had probably been ongoing privately among members of the department. Practically every department faculty and staff member responded expressing frustration, anger, and sadness at witnessing the tragedy. The department chair expressed similar outrage and offered me support. This email thread lasted three days with people presenting suggestions for reform and other ideas for creating change around systemic racism. By that time, one of the other library departments at City University of New York (CUNY) released a statement addressing its frustration and outrage at the George Floyd tragedy on the CUNY library listserv. The statement was both honest and practical in terms of presenting ways to educate people on the history of systemic racism in America.

The next day I received an email from my department chair asking if I wanted to draft a letter of response to the tragedy and share it among department members to have them add ideas. Knowing my department chair, who has proven to be a champion of causes that address racism, sexism, and xenophobia, I perceived her intent for asking me to draft the department response as a chance to address the issue from the lens of an African American male in America. I jumped at the opportunity and asked her to give me a couple of days to put a draft together. I used a quote from James Baldwin as the foundation for my statement. Baldwin, speaking about race in the documentary, "I heard it through the grapevine", stated, "What we are dealing with really is that for Black people in this country there is no legal code at all. We're still governed, if that is the word I want, by the slave code" (Fontaine & Hartley, P. 1982). My statement spoke to the history of systemic racism in America and how the murder of George Floyd was a public display of this history. After completing the draft, I emailed it to the department chair first to get her feedback and determine if it was "too real," and she approved of the brutal honesty of the statement and passed it on to the rest of the department for review.

The response from the library was overwhelmingly in favor of my draft. It sparked dialogue among the library staff, which resulted in the creation of a list of reading materials and resources that served to inform people how they could educate themselves on systemic racism and its ugly history in America. Although the letter didn't lead to new initiatives on the topic of systemic racism, the library's response was a bright spot in a truly traumatic time for me as both a Black man and a Black librarian. The library's response showed me that honest expression is the best way to address racism. The only way true change will ever take place around this issue is through honest conversations that can serve to educate others on the painful reality of being Black in America.

Conclusion

Each of the abovementioned libraries in PWIs responded to these social justice uprisings and activism with similarities and differences. Emory University, a liberal institution, is situated in Atlanta, a predominantly

Black city. These demographics, coupled with a Black library dean, set the stage for the quick, proactive approach that the library took in response to the social climate. On the other hand, TAMU and BMCC took a more passive stance that was more related to this one incident rather than acknowledging the systemic nature of police violence and institutional racism.

Another important similarity is that each of us used writing as a medium to explore, share, and stimulate discussions within our environments. Writing is known to offer cathartic effects that can reveal and heal those who engage in the process. Writing provided an outlet to engage our students, researchers, and colleagues. Emory Libraries' Racial Blog series was used to highlight the connection between the library and archival resources and present-day events. TAMU's library guide included Rebecca's Juneteenth essay and presentations on monuments and statues, which helped to uncover the troubling history of Texas and TAMU. Anthony's email and letter considered the personal and emotional toll of the racial upheaval in Summer 2020.

The differences in responses from the libraries in which we all work provided the latitude for our individual actions. Opening oneself up to colleagues can be difficult, but doing so laid the groundwork for important, hard conversations and facilitated direct actions on each of the campuses. Racism has long plagued America and is very much in existence and as Black librarians, we each participated in amplifying these issues both in our departments and in the profession overall.

Rebecca's presentation on Confederate statues, used in the archival institution's Summer Cushing Curator Talks, was the catalyst for many campus protests and discussions. Many institutions, governments, and organizations had been tackling the issue of Confederate monuments and statues for a few years with little movement. There hasn't been an *epiphany* to remove the Sul Ross Confederate statue on A&M's campus, but the attempt to ignore and distort this history is no longer possible.

Jina, as noted, worked under the leadership of a Black dean at Emory University's Woodruff Library who was invested in DEI issues, as well as a positive and safe environment for library employees. She proactively engaged her staff to create resources that promoted the library's materials in an effort to help the student body as they grappled with the racial climate that summer. The dean is committed to sustaining initiatives that she created and/or supported such as revising language in finding aids, creating anti-racist metadata, providing professional development around DEI issues, and maintaining space for Black library employees to convene. The dean's efforts prior to George Floyd's murder laid the groundwork for the swift and successful response in the aftermath of Summer 2020.

What has changed? More than a year since the death of George Floyd, there have been many more public killings of unarmed Black people recorded for the world to view. The marches and protests continued throughout the United States and all over the world with Black Lives Matter a rallying cry.

George Floyd's killer has been convicted of murder, but we wait for more police accountability and justice. This chapter highlighted the experiences and actions of three Black librarians and archivists who made concrete contributions in confronting issues of racism and white supremacy while encouraging change to our practices through a social justice lens in our perspective libraries. Our efforts manifested through leadership, professional motivations, and personal impact. Systemic issues will take more than a few years or a few people to bear any fruits of change. However, library and archival professionals can advocate for social change at their libraries and advance their own interests through a social justice lens.

References

Bruchko, E., DuVernay, J., & McGavin, M. (2020). *Emory Libraries Racial Blog Series,* https://scholarblogs.emory.edu/woodruff/tags/racial-justice-blog-series

Fandos, N. (2020, June 5). Frustration and fury as Rand Paul holds up anti-lynching bill. *The New York Times.* https://www.nytimes.com/2020/06/05/us/politics/rand-paul-anti-lynching-bill-senate.html

Fontaine, D., & Hartley, P. (Directors). (1982). *I heard it through the grapevine* [film]. Living Archives, Inc.

Hankins, R. (2021). TAMU: HIST 489: Black Lives Matter at Texas A&M, in Texas, & the world-Summer 2021 https://tamu.libguides.com/c.php?g=1132782&p=8267188

The Independent: Devoted to the consideration of politics, social and economic tendencies, history, literature, and the arts (1877).

Jones, D. (June 4, 2020). *Essentials of Cultural Competence.* DeEtta Jones & Associates.

Rivas Sullivan, C. (2019). Understanding the archivist's role in contextualization, removal, and relocation of confederate monuments at cultural heritage institutions. *Journal for the Society of North Carolina Archivists*, (16), 2–40. https://doi.org/10.17615/aym4-4n88

Texas A&M University's Commission Charge and Membership: "Commission on Diversity, Equity, and Inclusion," 2020: https://president.tamu.edu/messages/announcing-commission-charge-and-membership.html Retrieved October 18, 2021.

Texas A&M University's Core Values, January 2021: https://www.tamu.edu/about/coreValues.html Retrieved October 20, 2021.

Texas A&M University's A Report by the Commission on Diversity, Equity, and Inclusion, https://president.tamu.edu/committees-task-forces/commission-on-diversity-equity-and-inclusion/documents/CDEI_Executive_Summary_2021.pdf Retrieved October 18, 2021.

2 Community-Building, Empowering Voices, and Brave Spaces Through LIS Professional Conferences

Jennifer Masunaga, Aisha Conner-Gaten, Nataly Blas, and Jessea Young

This chapter will describe how four Black, Indigenous, People of Color (BIPOC) academic librarians conceived, planned, and executed a one-day in-person summit for BIPOC information workers in 2018 to provide an engaged and supportive space in Los Angeles, California. The original four organizers of the 2018 People of Color in Library and Information Science (POC in LIS) were Nataly Blas, Aisha Conner-Gaten, Jessea Young, and Rachel Deras. In 2019, Jennifer Masunaga joined the 2021 planning team upon Rachel's departure. We, the authors, would like to acknowledge the dedication and labor of Rachel Deras; the first summit would not have been a success without her.

To address why BIPOC-centered programs are vital to the success of the LIS field, this chapter will first examine issues of inequity in conference organization and whiteness in LIS in both conference content and planning. It will also describe the steps the summit organizers took to encourage conversations regarding inclusivity and accessibility in the profession. Lastly, it will discuss summit outreach to the public, school, and academic information workers as both presenters and attendees. Specific focus will be placed on cross-professional networking that invites all information workers into a shared forum. This invitation highlighted the unheard experiences of LIS information workers who normally lacked support to attend professional events. Practical suggestions for creating similar styled events will also be provided along with resources and lessons learned from the organizers, including the move to an online format considering the COVID-19 pandemic in 2020.

Understanding Brave Spaces

A critical step in creating socially responsive libraries is to secure, nurture, and protect the mental health and wellbeing of its Black, Indigenous, People of Color (BIPOC) information workers. Modern librarianship, information systems, and institutions have forever prioritized and normalized whiteness in public, academic, and archival spaces (Brook et al., 2015; Honma, 2005; Ossom-Williamson et al., 2020; Wheeler et al., 2004). Within these systems, BIPOC experience profound harm and are silenced for demanding action

DOI: 10.4324/9781003167174-3

to unseat oppression. As Brown et al. (2018) note, the isolation felt by many People of Color (POC) in LIS stems from an overarching emphasis on whiteness; how it is performed, how it is promoted above ethnic and cultural diversity, and how it is regulated through systems and administration (p. 178). To amplify and bolster siloed BIPOC, brave spaces have been organized by BIPOC themselves, often created by special interest groups within larger organizations (Anantachai et al., 2016, Echavarria & Wertheimer, 1997).

BIPOC-only spaces promote the resistance of oppression (e.g., sexism, racism, etc.) and allow the reclamation of BIPOC identity repressed in predominantly white workplaces (Blackwell, 2018). As April Hathcock (2016) so succinctly states:

> The fact is that people from the margins need safe spaces. We need places we can go to laugh, cry, scream, and shout among our own. We need exclusive spaces where we can curse our lot, speak our minds, and then dry our faces and take back up our fighting stances. We need places where we can be weak and vulnerable without being in danger or exposed.

However, when BIPOC-only spaces are formed and included in larger professional organizations, they can exclude the most vulnerable workers who cannot afford to pay dues and attend conferences.

Terminology

This chapter defines whiteness as the "normative and persistent cultural characteristics" of the white Western European culture (Brook et al., 2015) but also as an invisible "socio-cultural category" that is used to maintain the social-cultural status quo that privileges and works in favor of whites (Honma, 2005, p. 5). The organizers of the People of Color in Library and Information Summit use the terms "People of Color (POC)", "BIPOC (Black, Indigenous, People of Color)" and "library workers of color" as a way to incorporate all non-white library and information workers. We acknowledge these generalized terms each have their criticisms, but they are used here as a way to unify members of underrepresented racial and ethnic groups within LIS (Deo, 2021; Garcia, 2020; Grady, 2020; Meraji et al., 2020).

White Invisibility and Conferences

According to membership demographics of the American Library Association (ALA), librarianship in 1998 was 86% white and in 2017, that number had risen to 87% (American Library Association, 2017). Despite the existence of many programs for librarians of color, the lack of ethnic and racial diversity in librarianship has not improved, especially in academic libraries. As a result, academic librarians of color report feeling isolated, alienated, lonely, and frustrated by the overwhelming whiteness of the profession (Alabi, 2018, p. 135). The field has attempted to discuss its "diversity problem" by making changes to LIS curriculum, career programming, and recruitment and hiring practices (Hathcock, 2015; Jaeger et al., 2011; Tang & Adkins, 2017). However, LIS continues to maintain whiteness and does not interrogate how it reinforces and contributes to white racial normativity (Brown et al., 2018; Honma, 2015).

Fobazi Ettarh (2018) coined the phrase "vocational awe" to describe the view of libraries as an institution that is inherently good and politically neutral. When we frame the library as a politically neutral place, we are less inclined to see how librarianship is built on and upholds racial hierarchies and white dominant power structures. When LIS as a field discusses its "diversity problem", it is careful to avoid race or critiquing the profession and its institutions. In fact, as Schlesselman-Tarango (2016) notes, we conceptualize diversity as a racial difference with whiteness being the norm (p. 669). When gathering information workers at conferences, whiteness continues to pervade, leaving many POC information workers without recourse or community.

With whiteness being both invisible and the norm at LIS conferences, opportunities for authentic conversations about POC experiences remain elusive. A review of the history of ethnic professional associations within ALA shows that these groups were formed out of the racial segregation of Black, Asian and Latinx librarians from white conferences spaces (Echavarria & Wertheimer, 1997). Even when they were invited into larger, professional spaces, they found the unique needs of their own groups ignored or marginalized. Hathcock (2016) articulates the need for a space where POC community building is emphasized and justification for its value is not questioned by the dominant power. While the ethnic ALA caucuses and other groups are important partners in the lives of BIPOC workers, many of these groups are dedicated to the promotion of user services and programming. There are few conferences that are dedicated to addressing the personal and professional needs of BIPOC workers and even fewer that occur at the intersection between public, private, and school libraries and their diverse staff.

Counterspaces

One solution to POC lacking authentic dialogue on whiteness is the development of counterspaces or safe spaces to support and mentor other information workers of color. Often unaffiliated with professional associations and ethnic caucuses, Solorzano et al. (2000) developed the notion of counterspaces "as sites where deficit notions of people of color can be challenged and where a positive collegiate racial climate can be established and maintained" (p. 70). Furthermore, counterspaces are "sites of radical possibility" that ensure patterns of oppression are not reproduced in the setting (Case & Hunter, 2012, p. 70).

Academic counterspaces are especially important for scholars of color because the space allows attendees to foster their own transformative learning and envelops them in an environment, "wherein their experiences are validated and viewed as important knowledge" (Solorzano et al., 2000, p. 70). Case and Hunter state counterspaces challenge deficit notions through narrative identity work, acts of resistance, and direct relational transactions including self-enhancement (2012). Anantachai et al. (2016) argue supportive networks and mentorship are key components of retaining librarians of color in academia. Because counterspaces are dynamic, they provide a space from which to consistently challenge, grow, and transform ourselves in the process of building community with others (Morales, 2017).

2018 People of Color in Library and Information Science Summit

Planning the First Summit in 2018

Starting in 2017, within the walls of the William H. Hannon Library at Loyola Marymount University (LMU), we decided to produce our own counterspace. As coworkers and friends, we sought and found solidarity, humor, and a sense of peace in our own company, often collaborating and attending LIS events together to further our professional goals. Seeking to advance conversations about oppression in LIS that occurred during Slack channels at work, we attended *Pushing the Margins: Women of Color and Intersectionality in LIS Symposium* at UCLA in 2017. This symposium highlighted POC who contributed to the Litwin Press volume of that same name that explored "the experiences of women of color in library and information science rooted in black feminism, critical race theory, and intersectionality" (Joint Council of Librarians of Color (JCLC), 2018). While a book talk is not unique to LIS, the symposium's content and, most importantly, the prioritization of BIPOC voices was groundbreaking and informative to us. For inspiration, we also looked to the JCLC occurring in September 2018 that same year. JCLC, the joint conference hosted by ALA ethnic affiliates only takes place every four to five years. For many librarians of color, JCLC is the only time BIPOC information workers are not considered the minority in the space; it is a visible reminder of the possibility of a LIS without the specter of white supremacy. With this in mind, we met in October 2017 and envisioned an event in which attendees could workshop their research ideas, practice their presentations prior to JCLC, and foster personal, professional, and mentoring relationships. It is from these conversations that the theme, *Empowering Collaborations and Creating Brave Spaces*, was born.

Following the lead of the predominantly female *Pushing the Margins* symposium, we initially proposed a localized, women-only event. However, considering that LIS is already a female-dominated field, we decided that inviting all information workers of color would lend itself to more community-building opportunities. The organizers settled on the word "summit" to describe an empowered meeting where everyone is an equal and active participant depending on their needs. We reflected on our inspiration, *Pushing the Margins,* and concluded that because librarians of color were sharing space with white librarians, the symposium became a space for librarians of color to share trauma or to justify their presence for white librarians to recognize their humanity. From this experience, we understood that our summit was not an ideal place for white people or their allyship work. We decided this summit was strictly "our time".

Knowing that the summit would need to strike a different tone to address the importance of POC-only counterspaces, we spent several organizer meetings just drafting the mission. We knew it had to guide the difficult conversations, relationship building across LIS and external to academia, the building and retention of skills, and the expansion of professional research as we knew it. We recognized that any event held on occupied white, capitalist lands could not be inherently "safe" for BIPOC. Instead, we wanted to invite attendees to be "brave" at the summit and engage with their own identities and internalized feelings in these spaces.

In addition to creating a POC-only space, and in order to gain the institutional monetary support needed to host the summit, we considered how the summit would support research activity. Presenting at conferences is an important part of librarianship; however, there are many barriers for POC to attend and present at conferences including cost, time off, and travel. With this in mind, we solicited funding for our home institution (LMU) for full conference funding.

As academic librarians who attended the white-dominated conferences in LIS, we wanted to prioritize creating a supportive and inviting environment for all attendees. Conferences can be intimidating, especially if one does not have a peer to teach them how to navigate the space and conference processes. To counter the intimidation of the proposal process, we specifically reached out to graduate programs and mentorship programs to encourage new and non-academic librarians to share their work and experiences in any mode possible (POC in LIS, 2017). We texted, called, and emailed folks who expressed nervousness about their knowledge and skill. Lastly, we noted that library research about POC experiences, self-care, and wellness had historically been discouraged at professional association conferences. It was our intention to allow folks to expand upon and research those topics that are key to their livelihood, even if they were deemed unacceptable for inclusion in other LIS spaces.

Topics and Impact of the 2018 POC in LIS Summit

The summit welcomed 78 information workers representing over 40 institutions from 5 different states to LMU's campus. While the majority of
attendees were from academic institutions, there was representation from
public libraries and schools (see Figure 2.1). Additionally, the summit highlighted three first-time keynote speakers and seven first-time presenters
among a variety of presenters from various LIS areas (see Figure 2.2). After
participating in the summit, several presenters collaborated and presented
research at larger LIS conferences, including the Association of College and
Research Libraries Conference and JCLC, just as we intended.

The summit theme, *Empowering Collaborations and Creating Brave
Spaces*, inspired topics from self-care to research interests and peer support
systems (see Figure 2.3). Keynote speakers Nancy Olmos, Suzanne Im,
and Eva Rios-Alvarado from Librarians of Color Los Angeles (LOC-LA)
kicked off the summit with impactful narratives and a call to action. Their
keynote, *Holding the Center: The Evolution of Librarians of Color Los
Angeles* opened with spoken word and personalized poetry reflecting on
their histories and present. In the true spirit of grassroots activism and
creatively organizing in professional spaces, the keynote speakers then
invited attendees to contribute to a living document: scraps of cloth with

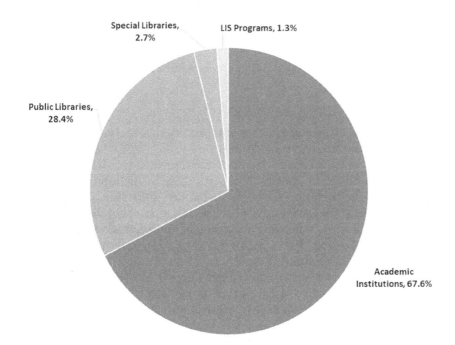

Figure 2.1 POC in LIS 2018 Summit Attendees by Institution Pie Chart

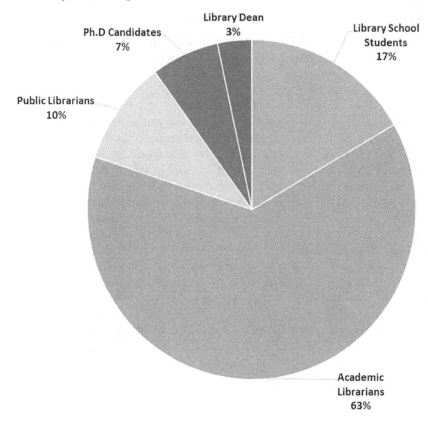

Figure 2.2 POC in LIS 2018 Summit Presenters by Profession Pie Chart

sayings, images, and thoughts to be stitched together and continued at the JCLC a few months later.

According to the summit's feedback survey, attendees listed personal growth & development, content, and networking as the top three reasons for attending the summit. When asked what they took away from POC in LIS Summit, the attendees stated they learned a new skill, learned about self-care, and created a network for personal and professional colleagues (see Table 2.1). Notably, the summit created space for information workers in diverse institutions and role types, often siloed at other conferences, to foster collaborations and share their experiences in LIS (Blas et al., 2019).

As one attendee noted, "I have never in my professional career been in a room full of beautifully diverse information professionals. I am part of a greater movement and our voices are powerful. That due to our determination, this profession is changing. Thank you for holding up a mirror to allow me to see dignity, grace, and strength within myself".

The POC in LIS Summit covered a range of topics:

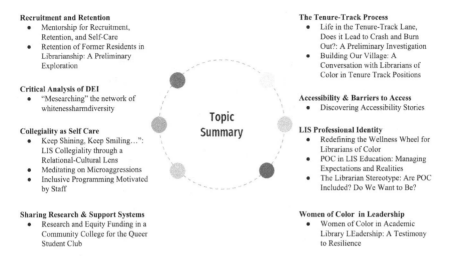

Recruitment and Retention
- Mentorship for Recruitment, Retention, and Self-Care
- Retention of Former Residents in Librarianship: A Preliminary Exploration

Critical Analysis of DEI
- "Mesearching" the network of whitenesssharmdiversity

Collegiality as Self Care
- Keep Shining, Keep Smiling…": LIS Collegiality through a Relational-Cultural Lens
- Meditating on Microaggressions
- Inclusive Programming Motivated by Staff

Sharing Research & Support Systems
- Research and Equity Funding in a Community College for the Queer Student Club

The Tenure-Track Process
- Life in the Tenure-Track Lane, Does it Lead to Crash and Burn Out?: A Preliminary Investigation
- Building Our Village: A Conversation with Librarians of Color in Tenure Track Positions

Accessibility & Barriers to Access
- Discovering Accessibility Stories

LIS Professional Identity
- Redefining the Wellness Wheel for Librarians of Color
- POC in LIS Education: Managing Expectations and Realities
- The Librarian Stereotype: Are POC Included? Do We Want to Be?

Women of Color in Leadership
- Women of Color in Academic Library LEadership: A Testimony to Resilience

Figure 2.3 2018 Summit Presentations by Topical Track Listing

Note: Reproduced from the 2018 POC in LIS Impact Report, https://digitalcommons.lmu.edu/cgi/viewcontent.cgi?article=1100&context=librarian_pubs

Table 2.1 Summit Attendee Feedback Survey Results: Did You Do Any of the Following Bar Chart. Reprinted from the 2018 Impact Report.

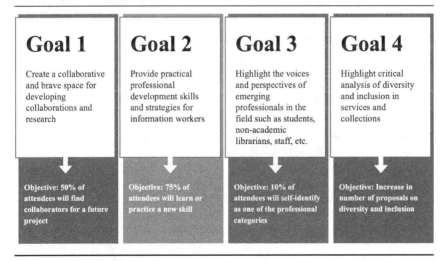

Goal 1	Goal 2	Goal 3	Goal 4
Create a collaborative and brave space for developing collaborations and research	Provide practical professional development skills and strategies for information workers	Highlight the voices and perspectives of emerging professionals in the field such as students, non-academic librarians, staff, etc.	Highlight critical analysis of diversity and inclusion in services and collections
Objective: 50% of attendees will find collaborators for a future project	Objective: 75% of attendees will learn or practice a new skill	Objective: 10% of attendees will self-identify as one of the professional categories	Objective: Increase in number of proposals on diversity and inclusion

Note: Reproduced from the 2018 POC in LIS Impact Report, https://digitalcommons.lmu.edu/cgi/viewcontent.cgi?article=1100&context=librarian_pubs

Identity Work at POC in LIS Summit

Identity work is the process by which individuals or collectives give meaning to themselves and others through narratives, which brings upon healing and restoration to marginalized groups (Case & Hunter, 2012). Several presenters shared narratives that validated the experiences of info workers of color to promote healing and restoration. For example, in *Mesearching: the network of whitenessharmdiversity*, presenter Joyce Gabiola explored the harmful nature of diversity work in LIS and the role of POC, from their own experience, in a profession embedded in whiteness (2018). Through their experience on diversity committees in LIS, Gabiola characterizes the power dynamics that stunt the possibilities of an anti-oppressive learning environment. In particular, Gabiola argued that diversity research was a panopticon to surveil POC, and diversity initiatives were institutional devices to control POC and protect whiteness. Their presentation was rated the second-highest rated session at the summit; tapping into the shared frustration over diversity committees and initiatives within libraries.

Resistance Narratives at POC in LIS Summit

The summit also provided space for resistance narratives which articulate the strength and capability of setting members to overcome and resist oppression (Case & Hunter, 2012). *Redefining the Wellness Wheel for Librarians of Color*, presented by Amanda Leftwich, defined the dimensions of wellness, barriers faced by POC in the workplace, and made recommendations for wellness in information practice (2018). This presentation was the first time Leftwich introduced this methodology to the field, which would later become a popular topic in LIS self-care practice.

There were two sessions on the tenure-track experience in academic libraries, *Life in the Tenure-Track Lane, Does It Lead to Crash and Burn Out?: A Preliminary Investigation and Conversation of Academic Librarians of Color Daily Experiences (Pun et al., 2018)* and *Building Our Village: A Conversation with Librarians of Color in Tenure Track Positions (Perera et al., 2018)*. The panelists of both sessions provided attendees with strategies for finding support, time, and mentors in the tenure process. Their frank discussions and answers allowed audience questions to finally find clarity with the oppressive and depressing academic processes we are required to endure.

The POC in LIS Summit as a counterspace provided information workers of color the opportunity to "think, feel and act in ways that are consonant with their own identities but that are typically devalued by the larger society" (Case & Hunter, 2012, p. 265). The summit provided social support through empathy, a shared sense of security, and less isolation (Case & Hunter, 2012). As one attendee wrote in their feedback survey, "... The funny thing is I attended to see how I could help contribute to this community; but you ended up helping me instead. I cannot say enough about my experiences here. Thank you for giving me the perspective I really needed, that I wasn't going to get anywhere else" (Conner-Gaten et al., 2018).

2020 People of Color in Library and Information Science Summit

Initial Plans for the 2020 POC in LIS Summit

Fueled by the positive feedback and impact, we were compelled to host another summit and decided on July 24, 2020. We considered the sustainability of the summit, particularly the importance of the low cost for presenters and attendees. In October 2019, the official planning for the 2020 POC in LIS Summit began including fundraising efforts to ensure financial stability. We brainstormed fundraising models and applied for and received funding from the Statewide California Electronic Library Consortium (SCELC) Project Initiatives Fund (SPIF) grant. Continuing our focus on community and how collaborations strengthen our own identities, we developed the 2020 Summit theme *Thriving Together: Strengthening Our Identities through Community.* We urged attendees to explore a specific thought question: *How can POC in LIS thrive together to create strong, diverse, and beautiful communities?* Following our experience as organizers in 2018 and due to our SPIF grant, we developed summit goals and objectives, with metrics to assess the impact of the event (see Figure 2.4).

Duplicating much of the planning used for the successful first summit, we developed an abridged timeline to ensure the success of the second summit (see Figure 2.5).

Addressing COVID-19 and Moving Online

Unfortunately, the COVID-19 pandemic disrupted the planning of the 2020 POC at the LIS Summit. Given the severity of the pandemic and remote

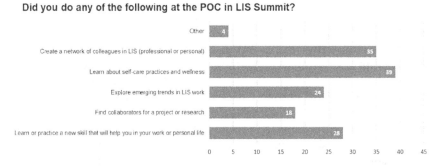

Figure 2.4 The 2020 POC in LIS Summit Four Goals and Outcomes

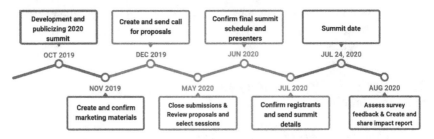

Figure 2.5 2020 Summit Timeline from October 2019 to August 2020

work requirements in early spring 2020, we decided to postpone the summit indefinitely. While this was a difficult decision, we wanted to retain the community-building spirit that was so valued by our attendees in 2018. As we began to grapple with the physical and psychological impact of COVID-19, we felt that there might be a need for the summit as a space for healing, grieving, and reflection. With that, an in-person summit was tentatively rescheduled for July 2021.

However, as the pandemic continued, we were forced to consider moving online or canceling altogether. There were benefits to an online summit as it would allow for more attendees unrestricted by the physical library space and invite global participation while maintaining free registration. Costs were also significantly lower with an online format. We could not dismiss the reduction of community building and peer networking that organically occurs in in-person events, as well as Zoom and remote work fatigue, and increasing competition from similar online events. But the benefits for this counterspace outweighed the disadvantages and in November 2020, the 2021 POC in LIS Summit moved online.

The Summit mission, theme, funding, planning, and outreach remained the same with the move online. We were able to also retain our funding which shifted our expenses to technology for presenters and increased presenter honorariums. The conference logistics, such as content, scheduling, and day-of technology needs, were re-evaluated for an online format. We brainstormed the best format to reduce Zoom fatigue and reviewed technologies to facilitate and improve the online experience. Given the importance of brave spaces in our mission, we adjusted the 2018 summit code of conduct including expectations for attendee behavior online during the summit. The code outlines and defines forms of harassment as well the consequences for those who engage in harassing or discriminatory behavior as well as a mechanism for grievance reporting. In the end, we decided not to record the Summit presentations. We knew that recording sessions could hinder open and honest conversations during the summit; which was critical to the success of the inaugural event. We also disabled the ability for attendees to download chat conversations from Zoom to protect the privacy of the attendees and to encourage open dialogue during the event.

Another key element of the initial summit was that of the POC-only space. We knew that others had achieved this online through rigorous protocol and gatekeeping and reached out for alternatives. To further strengthen this commitment, clear language was added to the attendee and presenter forms: "I understand the mission of POC in LIS Summit is to create a productive and brave space for people of color, especially women and marginalized identities, working in the information sector". This creates "a social contract" and community agreement among the summit organizers, presenters, and attendees to promote a productive and brave space.

The July 2021 Summit, as we hoped, brought together 124 attendees from 66 institutions online to share and uplift one another during one of the most difficult periods in our lifetime thus far (Blas et al., 2021). Organizers utilized four Zoom online conference rooms to host simultaneous tracks of 75 and 40-minute presentations, 30-minute roundtable discussions held in Zoom breakout rooms, and one, 2-hour optional workshop at the beginning of the conference in place of a keynote. Topics included parenting during the pandemic, the lived experiences of BIPOC administrators and leaders in academic librarianship, mentorships for BIPOC workers, and community archives of POC collections. With a 58% response rate to the satisfaction feedback survey, 98% of participants rated the online summit content as "good" or "very good", which we took as overwhelming satisfaction. As with most online meetings, we were concerned about screen fatigue and isolation but, with this feedback, it appeared most attendees were able to connect and participate in the counterspace successfully. It is our hope that future summits, whether online or in-person, achieve our mission, given our immense attention to building community, retaining trust, and, most importantly, providing a POC-only counterspace for all of our colleagues.

References

ACRL. (2021). *Registration*. The Association of College & Research Libraries Virtual Conference. https://conference.acrl.org/registration/

Alabi, J. (2018). From hostile to inclusive: Strategies for improving the racial climate of academic libraries. *Library Trends*, *67*(1), 131–146.

American Library Association. (2017). *2017 ALA Demographic Study*. ALA Office for Research and Statistics. http://www.ala.org/tools/sites/ala.org.tools/files/content/Draft%20of%20Member%20Demographics%20Survey%2001-11-2017.pdf

Anantachai, T., Booker, L., Lazzaro, A., & Parker, M. (2016). Establishing a communal network for professional advancement among librarians of color. In R. Hankins, & M. Juárez (Eds.), *Where are all the librarians of color? The experiences of people of color in academia* (pp. 31–53). Library Juice Press.

Blackwell, K. (2018, August 9). Why people of color need spaces without white people. *The Arrow*. https://arrow-journal.org/why-people-of-color-need-spaces-without-white-people/

Blas, N., Conner-Gaten, A., Deras, R., & Young, J. (2019). Empowering collaborations and creating brave spaces: People of Color in Library and Information Science Summit. *College & Research Libraries News, 80*(5), 270. https://doi.org/10.5860/crln.80.5.270

Blas, N., Conner-Gaten, A., Masunaga, J., & Young, J. (2021). "POC in LIS Summit 2021 impact report". *LMU Librarian Publications & Presentations, 131.* https://digitalcommons.lmu.edu/librarian_pubs/131

Brook, F., Ellenwood, D., & Lazzaro, A. E. (2015). In pursuit of antiracist social justice: Denaturalizing whiteness in the academic library. *Library Trends, 64*(2), 246–284. https://doi.org/10.1353/lib.2015.0048

Brown, J., Ferretti, J. A., Leung, S., & Méndez-Brady, M. (2018). We here: Speaking our truth. *Library Trends, 67*(1), 163–181.

Case, A. D., & Hunter, C. D. (2012). Counterspaces: A unit of analysis for understanding the role of settings in marginalized individuals' adaptive responses to oppression. *American Journal of Community Psychology, 50*(1–2), 257–270. http://DOI 10.1007/s10464-012-9497-7

Conner-Gaten, A., Blas, N., Deras, R., & Young, J. K. (2018). "POC in LIS Summit 2018 impact report". *LMU Librarian Publications & Presentations, 99.* https://digitalcommons.lmu.edu/librarian_pubs/99/

Deo, M. E. (2021, June 6). *Why BIPOC Fails – Virginia Law Review.* https://www.virginialawreview.org/articles/why-bipoc-fails/

Echavarria, T., & Wertheimer, A. B. (1997). Surveying the role of ethnic-American library associations. *Library Trends, 46*(2), 373–391.

Ettarh, F. (2018). Vocational awe and librarianship: The lies we tell ourselves. *In The Library With The Lead Pipe.* https://www.inthelibrarywiththeleadpipe.org/2018/vocational-awe/

Gabiola, J. (2018, July 13). *Mesearching: The network of whitenessharmdiversity* [Conference session]. People of Color in Library and Information Science Summit, Los Angeles, CA, United States. https://digitalcommons.lmu.edu/pocinlis/2018/schedule/6/

Garcia, S. E. (2020, June 17). Where did BIPOC come from? *The New York Times.* https://www.nytimes.com/article/what-is-bipoc.html

Grady, C. (2020, June 30). Why the term "BIPOC" is so complicated, explained by linguists. *Vox.* https://www.vox.com/2020/6/30/21300294/bipoc-what-does-it-mean-critical-race-linguistics-jonathan-rosa-deandra-miles-hercules

Hathcock, A. (2015). White librarianship in blackface: Diversity initiatives in LIS. *In The Library With The Lead Pipe.* https://www.inthelibrarywiththeleadpipe.org/2015/lis-diversity/

Hathcock, A. (2016, February 29). It's my struggle – give me space. *At the Intersection.* https://aprilhathcock.wordpress.com/2016/02/29/its-my-struggle-give-me-space/.

Honma, T. (2005). Trippin' over the color line: The invisibility of race in library and information studies. *InterActions: UCLA Journal of Education and Information Studies, 1*(2). https://escholarship.org/uc/item/4nj0w1mp

Jaeger, P. T., Subramaniam, M. M., Jones, C. B., & Bertot, J. C. (2011). Diversity and LIS education: Inclusion and the age of information. *Journal of Education for Library and Information Science, 52*(3), 166–183.

JCLC. (2018). *Pushing the Margins #JCLC2018 Extra.* The Third Annual Joint Conference of Librarians of Color 2018. https://www.jclcinc.org/conference/2018/pushing-the-margins-jclc2018-extra/

Leftwich, A. (2018, July 13). *Redefining the wellness wheel for librarians of color* [Conference session]. People of Color in Library and Information Science Summit, Los Angeles, CA, United States. https://digitalcommons.lmu.edu/pocinlis/2018/schedule/15/

Meraji, S. M., Demby, G., Escobar, N., & Devarajan, K. (2020, September 30). *Code switch.* https://www.npr.org/2020/09/29/918418825/is-it-time-to-say-r-i-p-to-p-o-c

Morales, S. (2017, June). "Re-defining counterspaces: New directions and implications for research and praxis". *Center for Critical Race Studies at UCLA Research Briefs 8.* https://issuu.com/almaiflores/docs/sm_counterspaces

Ossom-Williamson, P., Williams, J., Goodman, X., Minter, C., & Logan, A. (2020). Starting with I: Combating anti-blackness in libraries [withdrawn editorial]. *Leon S. McGoogan Health Sciences Library.* https://digitalcommons.unmc.edu/mcgoogan_articles/9

Perera, T., Murrain, S., Dozier, V., & Paloma Fiedler, B. (2018, July 13). *Building our village: A conversation with librarians of color in tenure track positions* [Conference session]. People of Color in Library and Information Science Summit, Los Angeles, CA, United States. https://digitalcommons.lmu.edu/pocinlis/2018/schedule/5/

POC in LIS Summit (2017). *POC in LIS Summit: Call for Participation.* People of Color in Library Information Science Summit. https://digitalcommons.lmu.edu/pocinlis/cfp.html

Pun, R., Carlos, A., & Kim, M. (2018, July 13). Life in the tenure-track lane, Does it lead to crash and burn out?: A preliminary investigation and conversation of academic LoC daily experiences [Conference session]. LMU Digital Commons, 2018, https://digitalcommons.lmu.edu/pocinlis/2018/schedule/4/

Schlesselman-Tarango, G. (2016). The legacy of Lady Bountiful: White women in the library. *Library Trends, 64*(4), 667–686.

Solorzano, D., Ceja, M., & Yosso, T. (2000). Critical race theory, racial microaggressions, and campus racial climate: The experiences of African American college students. *Journal of Negro Education,* 60–73.https://www.jstor.org/stable/2696265

Tang, R., & Adkins, D. (2017). Diversity in LIS education resources. *Journal of Education for Library and Information Science, 58*(4), 241–244. http://dx.doi.org/10.12783/issn.2328-2967/58/4/5

VanScoy, A., & Bright, K. (2019). Articulating the experience of uniqueness and difference for librarians of color. *The Library Quarterly, 89*(4), 285–297. https://doi.org/10.1086/704962

Wheeler, M., Johnson-Houston, D., & Walker, B. E. (2004). A brief history of library service to African Americans. *American Libraries, 35*(2), 42–45. http://www.jstor.org/stable/25649066

3 Information Is a Two-Way Street

How Libraries Can Learn from Community Outreach

Shaunda Vasudev

**Information Is a Two-Way Street: How Libraries
Can Learn from Community Outreach**

Social justice is about connecting people with the resources they need most: economic opportunities, health care, education, and housing. It is easy to say that everyone should have a fair shot at receiving these resources, but when inequities exist, how do we address the structural barriers? And how do we reach these marginalized communities as library workers? In this chapter, I will explain how I have sought to improve social justice through outreach and programming in my position as the Outreach and Engagement Librarian at Capital University. I will primarily focus on the relationship I have built with a student organization under the Office of Diversity & Inclusion. This organization is dedicated to bringing together women on campus, particularly women of color, to support each other in their academic, professional, and personal endeavors. As a woman of color, this was one of the first student groups I sought to work with and the relationship has been transformative for the library.

Many modern public libraries are engaged in social justice practices. From job help/placement centers to meal services, the library is prepared to provide for all users while building a community of families and young readers through early literacy programs. Social services have also been embedded within public libraries. Social workers are providing counseling on site and leading eviction prevention programs. In addition, many local public libraries provide free tax preparation and filing assistance, GED courses, English language & citizenship classes, and screen readers for the visually impaired. Public libraries are meeting people where they are and providing access to these services while presenting patrons with resources to further explore on their own. They are also advocating for more social justice awareness by selecting community reads like *Evicted* by Matthew Desmond and *Americanah* by Chimamanda Ngozi Adiche (Everybody Reads: Previous selections, 2021).

College libraries are unique in that they don't always have the same community buy-in. Academic libraries are still finding their place as

DOI: 10.4324/9781003167174-4

contributors to student success beyond the basics of study spaces, circulation, e-resources, and research assistance. Furthermore, as more institutions launch digital initiative programs and offer free devices to students, the library's computer areas will no longer hold the same value it did previously. EDUCAUSE Center for Analysis and Research (ECAR) found that "ninety-eight percent of students in the 2018 ECAR study reported using laptops in at least one class, and 94 percent of those surveyed regarded them as either very important or extremely important" (EIkins et al., 2020). Students have their own devices and are connected through campus wifi, thus reducing the digital divide, which is commonly defined as the barriers to accessing technology – owning devices, low bandwidth, having digital skills – all of which disproportionately affect communities of color.

Beyond improving access among students that do not own technology, the college library also houses helpful resources such as writing centers and career placement offices. Originally aligned with the principles of information commons, writing centers, and career placement services are standalone entities that share library space, without being fully integrated with library services. There are, however, opportunities for these areas to collaborate and offer programs like late-night study sessions with tutoring. Recently, Capital University's Career Development Center worked with the library to plan and host a program highlighting the career trajectory of a young local political candidate with progressive ideas and platforms on issues like ending economic segregation. Unfortunately, the program fell through due to a scheduling conflict, but a student organization was able to pick up where we left off and successfully hosted the speaker for a campus event.

When public libraries present adult programs, they're often collaborative experiences with strong community support. Within academic library spaces, a library program competes with other campus entities and their events. If another department or student organization is hosting a program at the same time, the campus library is competing for the same community members. Another thing to note is despite being housed in the same building, a writing center or career placement center event does not necessarily promote the library. These are programs within the library's space, unrelated to library services or information literacy. A student can leave from attending these programs still not knowing anything about the services and resources we offer.

Additionally, while some public libraries are offering mental health counseling services, a college campus has its own Wellness area that can provide supportive services and information. San Francisco Public Library became the first public library system to employ a social worker in 2009. As of 2020, "dozens of libraries across the nation have social workers on staff" (American Psychological Association, 2020). A college library has to partner with the Wellness Department to effectively incorporate these resources. Later, I'll share some of the ways we've been able to do this and include student organizations as co-sponsors. Student organizations connect with their peers in a casual nature and successfully share campus initiatives. Since our Center for Health & Wellness (CHW) performs outreach throughout campus, we're using the library's space as a visible location for receiving information on these services from other students.

Rethinking Library Programming

Fostering library participation in a college library setting can present challenges and requires patience. As the Outreach and Engagement Librarian, I connect the campus community to library resources using a non-traditional approach. I partner with different departments, providing library access points at campus events.

Recognizing that barriers exist to navigating academic resources in higher education is nothing new. By design, libraries are part of the dominant culture and can reflect those cultural norms including implicit bias (Tewell, 2019). The service desk can be intimidating thus limiting interactions among groups that have been historically alienated within society. Spatial designs also influence patrons' information-seeking behaviors as studies suggest "approaching the service desk for assistance was based on awareness of the availability and a patron's calculation of need weighed against the psychological and physical 'costs' of approaching the desk" (Pierce & Schilling, 2019). In other words, if one recognizes a service desk and decides to ask a question, will they leave with their needs met, or will they regret making the effort to interact? If a student feels that they will not be treated with respect and dignity, they are less likely to approach.

The library is embracing counterspaces and dismantling practices which makes library services intuitive to privileged classes while appearing inaccessible to marginalized groups. Counterspaces can be defined as spaces that help participants push back against demeaning ideologies and the microaggressions that derive from them, whether on individual or institutional levels (Lee & Harris, 2020). All students should feel comfortable using the library's space and asking library personnel anything. There should not be fear attached to asking questions due to a lack of awareness of the services we offer. One of my key tasks as a librarian at Capital University is working to expand equitable services and introduce the library as a safe space for students. I resist the idea that students should already know how to use library services, and so the library is actively creating a welcoming environment for all community members. Ultimately, when I participate in campus events, I am not just introducing students to our services, I am also personalizing the library's relationship with those students to remove any anxiety or feeling of not belonging.

My position specifically addresses the need for outreach with a focus on connecting with students from underrepresented groups at this institution. Prior to my arrival at Capital University, the library was rebuilding a full staff and no longer had an audience for programs. My first program was a Night at the Library event marketed to first-year students. It was promoted to departments and to first-year classes. It was a great event, reaching roughly 100 students on a Tuesday evening during the second week of classes. I used this fun event of food and games to introduce our services while providing a demo of the library's page with a Kahoot game and prizes. Students received a game card and won prizes for visiting different areas of the library. The local public library was also involved and distributed free Advanced Readers Copies (ARCs) of young adult novels to participants.

During the Night at the Library program, our director strategically encouraged library traffic from dismissed classrooms to join in on the fun program. Months later, after reflecting on low program attendance throughout the Spring semester with in-house programs, I finally recognized that an audience already existed with the numerous classes held in the library throughout the day. I began developing programs with these students in mind. Capital University's Department of Residential & Commuter Life included the library as a partner for a Wellness Week event where we had therapy dogs, a gaming night, and a zen space with adult coloring pages & free snacks. Residential Assistants (RAs), positions traditionally held by students, also helped market the program to their residents.

After the first year of programming, it was apparent that strong partnerships existed with various departments on campus. Academic Success and Career Development, both housed in the library, were always receptive to fresh ideas and collaborative opportunities. The Student and Community Engagement (SCE) Office remained a great resource for participating in campus events, and the Center for Global Education Department regularly welcomed the library's participation in classroom visits and social gatherings.

Through class visits with the Department of Education and attendance at events sponsored by the Office of Diversity and Inclusion (ODI), a student that frequented Capital University's library to study began asking the library to participate in events led by a student organization she was the president of The Global Student Association (GSA). This relationship was my gateway to closely viewing student programming. I was invited to International Expo Night, Culture Night, and facilitated a watch and discuss event with the movie *Bend It Like Beckham*. Many of these international students and GSA members were also regular library users. The Center for Global Education Department's leadership team remained an important partner in building this relationship by the consistent promotion of the library to its students. At least two librarians actively liaised and delivered classroom visits to this department within the past seven years prior to my arrival. The successful outcome of this collaboration was that library instruction and resources were now embedded in the Intensive English Language Program class. The Interim Director of the department contacted the library every semester to schedule research visits and consultations and include them in the course syllabus.

These initial attempts at building long-term relationships with students across campus did not always work out so smoothly. I had grand ideas and would work with my team to shape a library-themed experience, but the time and effort did not always result in student interest or participation. Students attracted students and as a library, we did not connect with a large enough audience to regularly promote a calendar of social engagement activities. Our in-house programs were hard to sell and attendance was extremely low. I didn't realize it at the time, but we were also competing against campus events led by students on campus. These events conflicted with general body meeting times held by many of the student organizations as well as their events.

That summer, I began considering the positive impact of student library workers taking on active roles in outreach efforts. Capital University's Department of Career Development & Academic Success were already using its peer advisors in campus outreach activities. After witnessing several successful tabling events with these advisors, it made sense for the library to proceed in a similar direction. So, I advocated for a student heavily involved with the ODI to be considered as a library student employee. This student had made a lasting impression coordinating the University's first-ever Diwali program and there was no question that they could also connect with a wider range of library users as a student library worker. Shortly after this student was hired by the library, they were assigned to co-host a library gaming program during Family Weekend. Due to her successful work marketing the program to her peers, the program saw a substantial increase in attendance from the previous year.

By personally inviting first-year students connected with the ODI to experience the library's gaming event, this new library student worker emphasized our space as a place where all students could feel comfortable. Libraries have been trying to improve services to underrepresented groups and be more intentional at creating programming for these communities. By building this bridge to encourage the use of this space by other students, the library is slowly breaking down this barrier. Eventually, this student, who remained connected with the ODI, would use their supervisory position as a Student Research Advisor to pay it forward and assist our efforts of expanding the library student worker team to include more diverse students that reflect the campus population.

After the first year of learning from successful and failed programming attempts, I set new goals to incorporate passive programming in the lobby area, partner with ODI-affiliated student organizations rooted in social justice practices, and share photos demonstrating library engagement on social media. Despite on-campus activity ending midway through the Spring semester due to COVID-19, the library was able to implement all three goals during the Fall semester.

The first lobby program of my second school year was a voter registration day and a Women's Suffrage Celebration with a button making activity led by two student organizations focused on women's empowerment: Sister Network and The Women's Empowerment Alliance (WEA). Sister Network is a student organization led by BIPOC female students and has supportive partnerships with Ebony Brotherhood Association (EBA) and the Black

Student Union (BSU). The WEA was a newer student organization, actively involved in promoting International Women's Day programs. Despite these two organizations sharing a similar focus, neither group had collaborated prior to the library's suffrage event. However, it was easy to elicit support from both organizations because three library student employees were members. The success of our voter registration and button making program can be directly attributed to the promotional efforts of these library student employees and the fact that the program was visible to library traffic. Prior to this, library programs were mainly held in classrooms, out of view of potentially interested attendees. During the program, students emphasized social justice themes by creating buttons with quotes from Sojourner Truth, highlighting important suffrage events, and including preferred gender pronouns.

Sister Network

I want to highlight especially the collaboration I've been able to foster with Sister Network (See Figure 3.1). This organization is dedicated to bringing together women on campus, particularly women of color, to support each other in their academic, professional, and personal endeavors. As a woman of color, this was an important group to work with and the relationship has been transformative for the library. Here's how that partnership was created.

In my first year at Capital University, the main outreach strategy involved working with Student Affairs and the Alumni Office to become more visible during campus events. I quickly learned to make friends on campus and join in various events. Later that fall, the library created a campaign to present research consultations off-site in the Athletics Center and the Student Union. Despite having only a limited number of interactions during these "drop in hours", there was one exchange with a student named Tate that proved to be extremely valuable in the long run. Tate was a member of various ODI student organizations and recognized me from a speed resources orientation event and a class visit. She used the "drop in hours" to discuss a research project and needed a refresher on locating articles for their upcoming assignment. For Tate, the interaction was more welcoming and did not produce the anxiety associated with asking questions at the library reference desk. When I first conceived of the idea of hiring our library's first student outreach assistant, Tate immediately emerged as a candidate because of her campus connections (she was the incoming president of Sister Network), her experiences as a library user, and her creative ideas for library programming.

Good Reads & Good Vibes

The summer of 2020 presented new challenges as libraries wrapped their heads around social distance practices and virtual platforms for Fall library programs. I was also the co-chair of the Programming, Outreach,

Figure 3.1 Meeting with Sister Network

and Marketing Interest Group (PROMIG) with the Academic Library Association of Ohio (ALAO) where my peer outreach librarians at academic libraries throughout the state were discussing this uncertainty and what library virtual programs would look like among our Slack group. As our new student outreach assistant, Tate discussed with me an idea for a virtual book club inspired by the recording artist Noname, whose popular book club was promoted heavily on her social media pages. She also discussed ways to restructure existing library programs to maximize student participation.

Our next event, Good Reads & Good Vibes, was a take on a Read-In program promoted the previous year during Black History Month. Tate and another student were the only attendees for the program during the previous year, despite marketing efforts through various campus outlets. As Tate and I planned for Good Reads & Good Vibes, we often discussed why the previous program did not draw a larger crowd. Learning from my past experience, Tate promoted this new program to the Sister Network members and other ODI student organizations through social media and, even more crucially, informal student networks. As a result, we had an incredibly strong turnout despite the event being virtual and during the evening hours. Good Reads & Good Vibes generated a very productive conversation focused on sharing favorite books and discussing disparities within the publishing industry.

A student shared what they loved about Michelle Obama's *Becoming* with post-it notes placed in the physical copy to mark areas they frequently returned to for inspiring messages. Another student discussed an upcoming self-publishing project they were working on exploring themes of colorism. Later in the program, another student shared their screen of a personal online library that rivaled what we had within our collection. It informed me of the continued work we need to do to expand our works by BIPOC authors.

I asked a general question around activist Fred Hampton's life and the holiday Kwanzaa: Why are there limited publications recognized as "scholarly" covering each of these two areas? One student agreed that this was an issue and expounded on what they learned through various outlets on the life of the holiday's founder. I wanted to get the students thinking about the frames "Authority is Constructed" and "Contextual and Scholarship as Conversation" (ACRL Board, 2016. Although these frames have been criticized for lack of learning outcomes related to social justice, they are still recognized for having "the potential to empower and transform library educators' approach to instruction and assessment" (Branch, 2019). With this conversation, we were addressing a disparity among "credible" works recognized in academia based on a biased approach to recognizing authoritative contributions in this area. One concrete result of this conversation is that the library at Capital University is now making a serious effort to promote books by BIPOC authors and focused on BIPOC themes, including having a display section. The library is also committing to spending more to address gaps in the collection of books relevant to marginalized communities.

The most successfully attended program was a Black History Month event inspired by a post on Noname's site promoting the film *Black and Cuba* directed by Dr. Robin J Hayes. We co-sponsored a discussion around the film with Sister Network, the BSU, and Students of Latinx Affinity (SOLA). Tate's relationship with leaders of other student organizations and my relationship with faculty and staff contributed to a healthy attendance for this Wednesday night program. The LGBTQ Pride group supported the night in solidarity with other ODI organizations and made a last-minute decision to cancel their program scheduled during the same time and reschedule for another week.

The discussion was facilitated by a Black female History professor and also included in attendance an Education professor (the only other Black tenured female faculty at Capital University) and the Chair of the World Languages Department who serves as SOLA's advisor. BSU's advisor, the director of IT and also a BIPOC female, attended as well to support the group and the conversation. It was a lovely night full of incredibly stimulating conversations. As I took notes and counted attendance during this virtual program, I couldn't help but to think how far the library had come in being able to generate this level of engagement from students, faculty, and staff in just two years.

Our last event of the year was a Women's History Month event with stamp making from a local Nigerian American textile artist. This event had been in the making since the beginning of the year, and we were excited to have it as the final event of Women's History Month. Sister Network assisted the Library in providing supplies and covering the presenter fee. Following a cue from GSA's successful Women's History Month program with many of the ODI organizations, we decided to promote the program on a campus marketing outlet instead of just on social media. Tate also reached out to individual Sister Network members to encourage attendance of this event. As a result, the program attendees not only included students but also three admissions staff members, including the Director of Admissions who serves as the advisor for Sister Network. We were also joined by several first-time attendees of library programs alongside student organization leaders. Thanks to Tate's contributions, we are now more visible to students not only as a space to study and do research but also as a collaborator on social justice-themed programs and initiatives. In my efforts to get the Capital University community, especially students, to engage with the library, I also learned a great deal about the needs and wants of the students and the ways the library can partner with them.

Campus Literacy and Student Success

Understanding that access points may be different for students of underrepresented groups, it's important to recognize that navigating the college experience and utilizing campus resources does not come naturally to certain populations. If the library can serve as an equitable place to promote these messages, it increases the likelihood that information will be communicated with other groups that normally would not engage in these services due to lack of awareness. Everywhere from registrar's info, financial aid, res, and commuter life initiatives can use this space as a hub in addition to promoting info within their departments and student union. Librarians are a resource for information and they can also be extended beyond research inquiries. This is how libraries can become more intentional in delivering their social justice message: equal access to all areas of campus.

While working with Residential & Commuter Life, it became apparent that commuter students were another group that may have looked to the library as a comfortable space to study between classes, but did not always connect with library services offered. How did these students connect with other departments? Were there barriers preventing them from accessing campus services offered from the Registrar's and Financial Aid offices that held business hours during the day? And how do we promote messages from vital departments that contribute to student success? Campus literacy became a tool in distributing these messages and expanding access by arming librarians and library student workers with the ability to talk about these various services at the front desk with first-hand knowledge and expertise. Although we may not be able to offer advising, we can certainly make sure that all students are aware this information is readily available and accessible within our library space.

In the fall of 2019, the library collaborated with the Center for Health and Wellness (CHW) to provide an information table in the lobby area. As the school moved toward incorporating wellness into the class syllabus, it was valuable to have the services highlighted around various areas of campus. The idea for the library partnership was born out of hearing a presentation delivered to campus faculty and staff by the director of the CHW.

Although student success encourages us to view students holistically, mental health is still incredibly stigmatized. Partnering with the CHW was a way to normalize the service and also make it visible to all students. Since I joined Capital University, I have regularly coordinated tabling events in the library on behalf of the CHW. The first tabling event was successfully led by a student intern within that department. In addition to Wellness info being offered, a library student worker tabled beside them, offering resources and asking visitors to complete a questionnaire. The questions ranged from knowledge around library classification systems for locating wellness items and awareness of the CHW's location and services. In addition to students tabling the event, snacks and giveaway prizes encouraged high student participation on a busy morning. One of the key things we learned from the survey is that a majority of respondents indicated that they had no knowledge of the location of the CHW building, which is right next to the library, or the services they offered. As a result, we have continued to do regular collaborations with the CHW, including more tabling events, promoting their events and services, and putting their marketing materials throughout the library.

Through the successful partnership established with Sister Network, the library later hosted a collaborative lobby program exploring diverse BIPOC titles covering a variety of wellness topics. By this time, the library had successfully hosted CHW for a lobby program earlier in the fall, so they were a consistent partner. When Tate learned of this partnership, she modified our November CHW event to highlight works by BIPOC female authors. These works featured poetry, cookbooks, yoga, and novels coinciding with the theme of wellness and self-care. Sister Network officially co-sponsored the event and promoted it in their IG stories and by word of mouth. A representative from the group tabled for the event and student library staff were active participants and promoters of the program. All participants received a coffee mug filled with treats along with CHW resource materials highlighting the process for scheduling appointments using telehealth services. Beyond this event, we continued to display these titles on library tables and used every opportunity to include them in our themed monthly displays such as MLK Day, Black History Month, and Women's History Month. The promotional materials provided to the library by the CHW are in an area surrounded by books that reinforce images of People of Color engaged in wellness practices (yoga, tai chi, cycling, cooking).

As information outlets (news, social media, online articles, etc.) continue to present a daily cycle of images and stories, it's important that students are armed with the ability to evaluate these sources. Library programming can be a great tool for delivering these messages outside of the traditional classroom setting. Although this may not have been the original intent of library services, we've been able to adapt and continue to evolve to meet the needs of our users. The latest library outreach project is a collaborative initiative supported by ODI. With the support of a neighboring archivist at Denison University and Capital alum, we are working to facilitate a student and alumni-driven project collecting memorabilia and photos from BIPOC students over the years. It's a narrative that hasn't been told through the eyes of students of color. This will also be an opportunity to engage students in archives and digital humanities work and have more discussions around incorporating social justice learning outcomes into the ACRL Framework.

Working with student organizations expanded our library's knowledge of how information cycles through campus to other students. It helped me rethink campus outreach strategies and involve more input from our student library team. They are exploring the campus and figuring things out without our help, so we as information specialists can learn from these behaviors and redirect our approach for delivering library services and instruction. Through partnering with several ODI student organizations on campus, the library was able to engage a diverse set of users who offered unique experiences and successful contributions to campus programming. We were also able to expand library access and encourage critical thinking around gaps in published works and offer another bridge to connecting with BIPOC community members and allies. The most valuable experience of all was learning from our students how to market and lead these programs while sprinkling in library messages during events. An audience that is often reluctant to explore campus spaces beyond specific comfortable and safe spaces now sees the library as an inclusive setting and a willing partner in their goals. This is how the library is embracing a culture of social justice and welcoming the opportunity to share these messages around equity and inclusion from student organizations.

References

American Psychological Association. (2020, April). Libraries as mental health hubs. *Monitor on Psychology, 51*(3). http://www.apa.org/monitor/2020/04/libraries-health-hubs

Association of College & Research Libraries Board (2016). *Framework for Information Literacy for Higher Education.* Association of College & Research Libraries (ACRL). Retrieved November 4, 2021, from http://www.ala.org/acrl/standards/ilframework

Branch, N. A. (2019). Illuminating social justice in the framework: Transformative methodology, concept mapping and learning outcomes development for critical information literacy. *Communications in Information Literacy, 13*(1), 4–22.

Elkins, S., Hwang, S., Kim, D., Manolovitz, T., Mueller, K., & Owens, E. (2020). What do you want from us? Evaluating student interest in technology-based services in academic libraries. *College & Research Libraries, 81*(5), 844.

Everybody Reads: Previous selections. (2021, September 7). Multnomah County Library. https://multcolib.org/read/everybody-reads-previous-selections

Lee, E. M., & Harris, J. (2020). Counterspaces, counterstructures: Low-income, first-generation, and working-class students' peer support at selective colleges. *Sociological Forum, 35*(4), 1135–1156.

Pierce, S., & Schilling, A. (2019). Removing the invisibility cloak: Using space design to influence patron behavior and increase service desk usage. *Journal of Access Services, 16*(2/3), 56–77.

Tewell, E. (2019). Reframing reference for marginalized students: A participatory visual study. *Reference & User Services Quarterly, 58*(3), 162–176.

4 LibGuides for Social Justice
Limitations and Opportunities

Stephanie Porrata

Introduction

LibGuides have traditionally been used by library workers to organize, share, and connect people with information and library resources for specific courses, across many disciplines, and on specific topics. The shift to using LibGuides to educate, address, and advocate for social justice action exemplifies how library workers are using available tools to become advocates and allies for change. This expands upon the chapter author's previous work that questions whether LibGuides are meaningful and/or have an impact on the issues they address (Porrata, 2020). Specifically, what should creators reflect upon and what actions to take before publishing social-justice-focused guides. Using a combination of literature and other institutions' case studies, this chapter will: (1) highlight both the opportunities and limitations of LibGuides as a platform for social justice action and advocacy and (2) help LibGuide creators reflect critically on the motivations going into and the implementations of guides.

Background

LibGuides and Social Justice

Little scholarly work has directly examined the use of LibGuides to address social justice issues. The exceptions to this oversight are the works of Pagowsky and Wallace (2015) and Kostelecky (2018), authors whose publications directly address and provide examples of using LibGuides to address social justice issues. Sullivan et al. (2016) provide yet another example. These authors very briefly documented the development of their "Teaching #blacklivesmatter" LibGuide, explaining the context of their guide's creation, the objectives of their guide, and the types of resources included within. The works of Kostelecky and Pagowsky and Wallace (2015) will be discussed in further detail as case studies. The chapter author has been unable to find other examples of in-depth peer-reviewed literature that discuss the use of LibGuides to address social justice issues directly and

DOI: 10.4324/9781003167174-5

welcomes readers to share examples the author may have missed. On the other hand, there is lively discourse on Twitter that addresses the use of LibGuides for equity, diversity, inclusion, and social justice. The Twitter discourse captures a shift in attitudes about the emergent uses of LibGuides in this way, starting with a sense of urgency to share resources and educate about specific topics, gradually moving toward a more critical attitude toward these types of guides.

As the conversation around police brutality against unarmed Black Americans peaked again in May and June of 2020, discourse by "library Twitter" (referring to spaces used by library workers on the platform) was heavily grounded in resource sharing. For example, Kaetrena Davis Kendrick started a thread asking librarians to provide links to any anti-racism LibGuides they created in response to current events. As of March 2021, the thread has 38 direct replies, 191 retweets, and 316 likes with links not only to LibGuides but also to padlets and other resource guides (2020).

A couple of weeks later, Stewart tweeted the following:

> I am pushing hard in my (academic) institution right now about the privilege of education: to what extent do we, as information professionals, use our position in education (i.e. "let's share more resources!") in order to defend ourselves against the need for more direct action?
>
> (2020)

Stewart was reflecting on the context of antiracist library classification, pushing against the narrative that reading literature is enough for library workers to enact an antiracist library classification. In this thread, Stewart later suggested that there must be more direct action rather than passivity. In other words, more must be done than merely creating and sharing resources about antiracism, police brutality, Deferred Action for Childhood Arrivals (DACA), or any other social justice issue.

Moving into 2021 and coming off the January 6 insurrection on the United States capitol, librarians critically questioned the professional impulse to create LibGuides. For example, Kendrick replied to a Twitter thread started by Eamon Tewell with a suggested research topic: "'Let's Make a LibGuide': Research Guide Labor as Whiteness & White Privilege Deflection: A Study" (2021). Tewell followed up on Davis' reply with "oh no, don't get me started on libguides. But maybe … a list of links on a page will sort everything out this once?" (2021). Farkas (2021) also replied to this thread with an example of a colleague's impulse to contextualize current events through a LibGuide without acknowledging that context is not needed so much as a solution or action. Farkas follows up by asking who these guides are actually made for: students or other librarians?

Are LibGuides, then, an inappropriate tool for social justice advocacy and education? Or is the debate more complicated than such a tweetable question implies? LibGuides are tools, and tools are about how they are used, and usage requires action. Creating a tool can itself be a helpful action, but a solution requires the action of using the said tool. Yet, still, discretion must also be used to determine when LibGuides are the right tool in the first place.

LibGuides as Reading Lists

In the panel (Not) Another Anti-Racist Reading Group: From Discussion to Action, Caldwell remarks that reading groups/reading lists and LibGuides are low impact, low effort, low-cost band-aids that perpetuate the idea of a single answer to complicated social issues (Rood et al., 2021). Cooke (2020), Jackson (2020), and Muhammad (as cited in Aviles, 2020) share the sentiment that reading lists are more lip service than community care. All three authors leverage additional critiques against the creation and dispersion of antiracist reading lists and against the tendency of such feel-good lists to conflate the act of reading with the reality of taking action. These critiques apply to LibGuides because, while varying in their content and structure, many function indirectly as reading lists. Furthermore, critiques of reading lists are critiques of creating reading lists or, in this context, LibGuides.

Cooke (2020) provides a framework for how one might approach becoming an antiracist, outlining three steps: (1) critical self-reflection, (2) critical consciousness, and (3) action and advocacy. Reading lists are situated only in her critical self-reflection step (2020, para 13), suggesting that, to make a substantial difference, there is additional work to be done beyond creating and sharing reading lists. Cooke pushes against relying solely on reading and reading lists as an answer to racism or becoming an antiracist because "[j]ust reading without acknowledging the historical context and your own personal experience is merely indulging a trendy topic, or assuaging your guilt. Just reading allows you to check a box and say 'all done, I'm antiracist!'" (2020, para 5). Jackson, in line with Cooke, observes that the label antiracist "suggests something of a vanity project, where the goal is no longer to learn more about race, power, and capital, but to spring closer to the enlightened order of the antiracist" (2020, para 7). In a similar vein, Muhammad adds that the kind of enlightenment brought about by reading is short-lived and usually results in no further action from the reader (2020, para 12). LibGuide creators must go beyond approaching their guides as a box to be checked as a step toward enlightenment while remaining mindful that creating a LibGuide could perpetuate inaction in self-satisfied guide users.

Returning to the context of Stewart's tweet in the previous section, the instinct of some library workers to create LibGuides in response to social justice movements can be seen as creating a shield against "more direct action" (2020). The aforementioned authors argue that restricting one's action to reading all the antiracist texts on a booklist but going no further provides a false sense of accomplishment and enlightenment. Individuals and the institutions they belong to should be wary of creating LibGuides that perpetuate the idea that social justice advocacy is something to be checked off a list.

Going further, Jackson levies that reading lists lack pedagogy. According to Jackson, a list of texts alone "seldom instructs or guides" (2020, para 4), and those who ask for an antiracist reading list "can hardly be trusted in a self-directed course of study" (2020, para 6). This critique is especially relevant when LibGuides are used as pedagogical tools. LibGuide creators must, instead, ask themselves how to infuse critical pedagogy into their guides—a pedagogy responsive to the topic of the guide.

These critiques are not to diminish the role which being an educator and resource-gatherer can have within the context of social justice advocacy (as later demonstrated by Iyer's social change roles), but library workers must remember that action must not begin and end with the creation of a LibGuide, especially if it is primarily composed of a reading list.

Social Change Ecosystem Framework

Deepa Iyer, through her Social Change Ecosystem Framework, demonstrates that there is not one single way to participate in making a difference. Iyer (2020) proposes ten possible roles that a person can play in pursuit of equity, liberation, justice, and/or solidarity based on their own values and context: weavers, experimenters, frontline responders, visionaries, builders, caregivers, disruptors, healers, storytellers, and guides (p. 4). Library workers overlap in terms of what roles they fill, but, ultimately, roles are individual. Iyer also provides reflection questions that can be used to understand which role(s) an individual tends to take on, where there is potential for growth into and beyond said role(s), and what role(s) it is that one wants to take (2020). Reflection is key to this framework. Looking at advocacy through LibGuides using Iyer's framework—as an extension of roles— shows that being reflective and intentional about actions taken is just as important as the action taken itself.

Iyer goes on to discuss transformative versus transactional solidarity and how the former can push advocacy further. According to Iyer, transactional solidarity is "like being a spectator and a bystander or a mildly interested participant" (para 6), giving the example of going to a #BlackLivesMatter protest, taking pictures, going back home, then posting the images to social media. Iyer contrasts this with transformative solidarity, which "requires us to challenge ourselves [...] to figure out what we are willing to risk, to deepen relationships rather than walk away when they become hard, to commit for the long-term, and to disrupt the status quo" (para 6). For the previous #BlackLivesMatter example, transformative solidarity could look like any or all of the following:

> I persuade two friends to go to the march with me. I engage in a personal educational process to learn about the historical and ongoing effects of

white supremacy. I organize a session in the race/faith community I belong to about how we too perpetuate anti-Black racism and why we must stop. I build relationships with Black Lives Matter leaders in my city to extend my support. I show up time and again for the events they hold with new people in tow who take similar actions.

(para 4)

Both Iyer's Social Change Ecosystem Framework and concepts of trans-actional and transformative solidarity indicate that a space exists for LibGuides in personal and professional social change ecosystems. The dif-ficulty comes in determining whether the creation of a particular LibGuide is transactional or transformative. When creators understand their role(s) before creating guides, and when creators invest in self-reflection and a deep understanding of a community's context, guides are improved, and social justice becomes possible.

Framework for Social-Justice-Focused LibGuides

Digging deeper into using LibGuides as a tool for social justice education and advocacy, Twanna Hodge lists considerations in her Springshare blog post "Using LibGuides to support racial justice & create inclusive commu-nities" (2020). Hodge's blog post is the framework in which the following case studies are explored as well as built upon later.

Hodge asks the following three questions: (1) What can LibGuide owners provide that non-BIPOC creators tend to overlook? (2) How can LibGuides be built to make all users welcome and promote inclusivity? (3) How can LibGuides be used to start, continue, and move the conversation forward and into action? Hodge follows each question with a set of suggestions or considerations for that question. While Hodge's blog post addresses racial justice, the strength of Hodge's questions is that they can be applied to any type of guide, not just those created to educate about current events and social justice. Guide creators who want to create a social-justice-focused guide are invited to reflect beyond a checklist of questions and suggestions, but, at least with Hodge's post, creators have a sound place to start.

Case Studies

Pagowsky and Wallace (2015) and Kostelecky (2018) provided the only examples of traditionally published literature the chapter author found that addressed the motivations, considerations, and process behind mak-ing social-justice-focused LibGuides in a comprehensive way. Because of this, these cases have deeply informed the chapter author's approach to and interpretation of the topic. Of course, as the resources are lim-ited, so is the framework, leaving much room for further development. Furthermore, while these cases were written prior to Hodge's suggestions, these suggestions overlap a great deal with the decisions made by the case authors, demonstrating the care and reflection that went into each guide.

University of Arizona

In response to the #BlackLivesMatter protests of 2014, Pagowsky and Wallace (2015) created their "Ferguson Resources" LibGuide (now titled "Black Lives Matter Resources"). The authors' main goals were to support information needs regarding current events, support faculty who wanted to incorporate these issues into their courses and situate the library as an ally on campus (p. 1).

Returning to Hodge's first question about resources that non-BIPOC LibGuide creators tend to overlook, Pagowsky and Wallace almost directly address this: "We set out to collect a variety of resources—news, statistics, scholarship, literature, blogs—[...] from a variety of perspectives, particularly those that are not as frequently heard" (p. 197). There was intent to include resources of underrepresented persons, and they also included resources outside of what students might expect to find on a campus LibGuide (e.g., blog posts, social media, multimedia content). The authors also provided examples of projects and initiatives as well as links to organizations and organizers for guide visitors, which is in line with what Hodge suggests.

Not only did the authors show intent about what voices and types of resources to include, but they also showed mindfulness of the way these resources might perpetuate bias. The authors mitigate this bias through their information literacy courses with students:

> We teach our students more abstractly about the necessity of investigating bias through information literacy instruction ... Mainstream media often depict people of color as criminals (especially when compared to whites), regardless of if a crime has been committed, and even Google search results based on "relevance" invoke harmful stereotypes of people of color... Positioning biased perspectives about people of color as value-free, authoritative, and anything but a source that requires further investigation is detrimental.
>
> (p. 198)

By addressing the ways these resources might perpetuate bias, the authors make use of their LibGuide as a teaching tool, allowing it to do work beyond just its creation.

As for Hodge's question about building guides to promote inclusivity, while this article did not address how the authors built-in accessibility and inclusivity directly, a case can be made that the creation of the LibGuide itself was intended to promote inclusivity on campus. According to the authors, an aspect of this guide's creation was to demonstrate the libraries' allyship to their highly diverse campus community, "providing students—students of color in particular—with another safe space on campus" (p. 196). Many of Hodge's questions may not be answered directly by reading the content of the guides but by how creators articulate the impact and utility of their social-justice-focused guides.

Regarding Hodge's last question on starting, continuing, and moving conversations to action, Pagowsky and Wallace's LibGuide demonstrated how the creation and use of this LibGuide was collaboration and campus-community focused. The guide "opened the door for more partnerships on campus, and has hopefully laid a foundation for further collaboration with faculty in the realm of critical pedagogy and social justice" (p. 199). The authors note that they were intentional about asking for feedback from faculty members and student groups and that they were also asked to provide support for the Black Life Matters conference being hosted by faculty in the Africana Studies and Gender and Women's Studies Departments (2015). Such a conference about and for the communities addressed in the guide reflects a very tangible event sprouting from a campus-wide conversation.

Social-justice-focused LibGuides grow in power by being more collaborative, rooted in critical pedagogical approaches, and conscious of their reach beyond the library.

University of New Mexico

Kostelecky (2018) created a LibGuide centering Native American and Indigenous perspectives regarding the Dakota Access Pipeline and the #NODAPL movement. She aggregated first-hand accounts and relevant information to the #NODAPL movement, arguing that her guide acts as a new type of scholarly communication for Native American and Indigenous Knowledge.

In reference to Hodge's first question about resources that non-BIPOC LibGuide creators tend to overlook, Kostelecky's guide highlights the importance of including community-created content and content that lives outside of library collections—both of which tend to be overlooked. According to Kostelecky, a major motivation for creating this #NODAPL resource was to highlight the voices of Indigenous and Native peoples. Such voices are often excluded from mainstream media coverage (p. 2), heightening the crucial and revolutionary importance of including their work in this LibGuide.

Kostelecky showed intentionality about what information was being aggregated on this LibGuide—much of which lives outside of the library's collection. For example, Kostelecky included the cartoons created by Ricardo Caté, a local Native American artist, stating that "excluding it would have been a glaring omission obvious to our campus and tribal communities" (p. 9). The inclusion of this artist also demonstrates a deep understanding of those for which this guide was created: a community that engages with a variety of mediums.

Furthermore, the LibGuide includes material outside of what may typically be considered "scholarly", featuring resources that some guide creators might deem irrelevant or inappropriate. Kostelecky's work normalizes and validates this kind of information, establishing it as a form of scholarly communication because, "[b]y curating and selecting social media sources for guides or other instructional materials, libraries and librarians recognize and demonstrate to others that these formats are another valuable place to gather information" (p. 12).

In building a guide to promote inclusion, Kostelecky distinctly decided to stray from the traditional LibGuide structure. According to her, traditional guide structures rely on academic jargon to establish authority (books, databases, scholarly articles, etc.), creating barriers through a language that did not match the target audience for this LibGuide (p. 8). Instead, she opted for "News and Articles, Historical Background, Tribes and Organizations, Cartoons by Ricardo Caté, and Media" (p. 8), choosing texts and modalities able to reach a much wider audience.

Finally, in terms of impacting the current discourse around the pipeline, Kostelecky's motivation was to start and continue the #NODAPL conversation from the perspectives of Native and Indigenous people, highlighting community-created content to both fill in the gaps left by mainstream media (p. 2) and create a resource by and for the community. Ultimately, Kostelecky aimed for the DAPL LibGuide to act as a new form of scholarly communication for Native and Indigenous Knowledge, changing the idea of what scholarly communication must be, who is included, and how it might transcend the limitations of tradition.

And what of the importance of the relationship between creators and the LibGuide's topic? Kostelecky laid out how their identity played a role in the need for and the approach to this guide (pp. 2–3). Such full disclosure of both curators and contributors of such a resource only strengthened their guide.

Discussion

In this chapter, Hodge's questions have been utilized to evaluate two LibGuide cases. The interpretation of Hodge's questions and the case's answers differed because of differing local contexts as well as the differing prior knowledge, goals, and motivations of each author. The relationship between the authors and the topic of their LibGuide matter, too. Pagowsky and Wallace were outside of the community being addressed while Kostelecky was within the community being addressed. One's distinct orientation plays a role in their approach. These two case studies demonstrate that there is no universal way to make an effective LibGuide that tackles social justice issues. They also demonstrate how reflecting on purpose informs what is included, who is included, and how to measure impact. While the case studies were not looked at through a critical lens in this chapter (for the sake of brevity), they are also not above critique.

Critiques of Using LibGuides for Social Justice Advocacy

Social-justice-focused LibGuides can be low-impact and transactional if made in a vacuum. Social justice issues are community issues, and they should be addressed in collaboration with the represented community as well as with those in the campus community who have expertise in the specific area. Using a "yes, and" approach demonstrates going beyond creation into action. For example, "yes, I will make a LibGuide about DACA for our campus, and I will make sure to introduce this resource to my colleagues in the multicultural center". Keeping a guide relevant to the community and up to date is important.

LibGuide creators themselves can also be a limitation. Each creator carries their own identity and experiences into their work, and, as stated previously, whether they are within or outside the community being discussed can set the trajectory for the guide. Excellent guides should therefore be collaborative. Many eyes can help ensure things are not being left out or misrepresented. One caveat is that LibGuide creators should be mindful about approaching BIPOC, LGBTQIA+, disabled, or other historically marginalized groups about assisting with a LibGuide. People with identities under siege cannot or may not be able to spend the emotional and physical labor to help. Defining the purpose and goal of LibGuides beforehand can allow creators to reflect on how members of a specific community can best offer their input while limiting the amount of labor and harm being asked of them.

Creation of a LibGuide should expand beyond learning. If a guide is nothing more than a reflection of a creator's learning, the guide risks treating engagement with an issue as a box to be checked. A creator must mitigate as much harm as possible. A seemingly finished LibGuide is still incomplete without accompanying action.

Guiding the Creation and Implementation of LibGuides

Taking into consideration the literature, the critiques, and the case studies, this chapter adds two more types of reflection questions to Hodge's list:

- What should be considered before making this guide?
- How much do you know about the issue being discussed?
- Your identities and perspectives
- Are you part of the communities affected?
- Your local context
- Do you know anyone currently working in this space/doing work to advocate for a group/cause? What is your relationship with this group?
- What are you trying to accomplish with your guide?
- Are you trying to introduce a topic?
- Are you trying to reach a specific audience?

- What should be considered after making this guide?
- How does the guide stay relevant in your community?
- What kind of maintenance will this guide need?

In both case studies, the authors give a sense of how much they know about the specific topic being addressed and how that impacted their approach to their LibGuides. Reflecting on this question should help guide creators better comprehend why they are making a particular LibGuide. The identity of each author also played a part in how each guide was approached. Reflecting on one's identity within (or outside) the impacted community will help guide creators to be mindful of what voice to use when discussing a topic. For example, there is a difference between talking as an ally and talking as an affected person. Identity within or outside a community also helps inform what types of sources should be included. If the creator's experience is outside of what is discussed in the guide, there is even more reason to seek out overlooked resources.

A LibGuide's creator must reflect on local context when deciding whether to create a social-justice-focused LibGuide. After all, local context informs the need for such a guide in the first place. By reflecting on one's relationship with one's community and working as (and with) advocates and activists, a guide creator can make an informed decision about whether the guide fits into the social change ecosystem of the community. The creator may learn they would have more of an impact working with an advocate in a different capacity. For example, for a guide about DACA, if the creator has never spoken to a DACA recipient or with those who support DACA students on campus, the creator should foster those relationships before considering creating a guide. While a guide can serve as a means for connection after it is created, the most effective guides are by creators who have established relationships prior.

After a LibGuide is created, there is then the question of maintenance and relevancy. Having a maintenance plan to keep a guide current and relevant is key when addressing contemporary issues because the landscape is ever-changing. Relevancy can also extend to the guide itself. It is important to find opportunities to use the guide—whether through a regular partnership with a professor, campus office, etc.—to take further action.

Conclusion

In the face of social injustice, how can a LibGuide make a meaningful difference? Creating guides for social justice advocacy can be an appropriate and transformative part of library workers' social change ecosystems as demonstrated by the two case studies. However, there is much for LibGuide creators to reflect on before, during, and after creating a LibGuide that can mean the difference between a transformative and transactional guide. The purpose of a guide and the knowledge, identity, perspectives, and local context of its creator are just some of the reflections that can be done to inform transformative work. Just the act of making a LibGuide can be transformative in some contexts, yet, in many other contexts, making a LibGuide is just a starting point.

If you have decided that creating a LibGuide is the most appropriate course of action, the chapter author calls you to take the aforementioned "yes, and" approach to further your work through additional action. For example, after saying yes to making a guide, share it with a relevant campus office or community, build a curriculum around the guide, or pair your guide with a community event. Understand that your guide is a living organism, dependent on the community that it serves. Rather than solely answering the reflection questions posed by Hodge and this chapter, think about your own personal contexts and to ask questions that are most relevant to them. Make this a collaborative discussion with colleagues and the community whenever and wherever possible. Even the creation of this chapter itself should lead to something more, and the author has likewise called herself to take further action.

References

Aviles, G. (2020, June 5). "Reading as resistance? The rise of the anti-racist book list". NBC News. https://www.nbcnews.com/pop-culture/pop-culture-news/reading-resistance-rise-antiracist-book-list-n1225661

Cooke, N. (2020, June 19). Reading is only a step on the path to anti-racism. Publishers Weekly. https://www.publishersweekly.com/pw/by-topic/industry-news/libraries/article/83626-reading-is-only-a-step-on-the-path-to-anti-racism.html

Farkas, M. [librarianmer]. (2021, January 7). *When one of my colleagues yesterday suggested creating a LibGuide to "contextualize" what is happening for our students (white women* [Tweet]. Twitter. https://twitter.com/librarianmer/status/134724993 7357049858?s=20

Hodge, T. (2020). Using libguides to support racial justice & create inclusive communities. Springy News. https://buzz.springshare.com/springynews/news-49/libguides-tricks

Iyer, D. (2020, November 20). Beyond hashtags and slogans: When solidarity becomes transformative. Building Movement Project. https://buildingmovement.org/blog/beyond-hashtags-and-slogans-when-solidarity-becomes-transformative/

Iyer, D., SolidarityIs & Building Movement Project. (2020). Mapping our roles in social change ecosystems. https://buildingmovement.org/wp-content/uploads/2020/06/Final-Mapping-Ecosystem-Guide-CC-BY-NC-SA-4.0-Handles.pdf

Jackson, L. M. (2020, June 4). What Is an Anti-Racist Reading List for? Vulture. https://www.vulture.com/2020/06/anti-racist-reading-lists-what-are-they-for.html

Kendrick, K. [Kaetrena]. (2020, June 3). *Please add your #Antiracism #libguides to this list: [Tweet]*. Twitter. https://twitter.com/Kaetrena/status/12682073117865656 39?s=20

Kostelecky, S. R. (2018). Sharing community created content in support of social justice: The Dakota access pipeline libguide. *Journal of Librarianship and Scholarly Communication, 6*(2), 2234. https://doi.org/10.7710/2162-3309.2234

Pagowsky, N., & Wallace, N. (2015). Black Lives Matter!: Shedding library neutrality rhetoric for social justice. *College & Research Libraries News, 76*(4), 196–214. https://doi.org/10.5860/crln.76.4.9293

Porrata, S. (2020, October 27). *LibGuides for social justice: Transformative or transactional.* Academic Library Association of Ohio. https://2020.alaoweb.org/posters/social-justice

Rood, M., Sawyer, S., Caldwell, D., & Thacker, J. (2021, February 1). (Not) another Anti-Racist Reading Group: From Discussion to Action [Panel]. *Association of Southeastern Research Libraries*, Greensboro, North Carolina.

Stewart, M. [LeonStewart]. (2020, June 22). *I am pushing hard in my (academic) institution right now about the privilege of education: to what extent do we,* [Tweet]. Twitter. https://twitter.com/MLeonStewart/status/1275145910146805760?s=20

Sullivan, M., Anusasananan, C., & Ramos, T. (2016). #blacklivesmatter: The journey of a grassroots LibGuide. *CSLA Journal, 39*(2), 16–17.

Tewell, E. [EamonTewell]. (2021, January 7). *This, and how white supremacy & capitalism operate in conjunction to ensure everyone just gets back to work immediately to* [Tweet]. Twitter. https://twitter.com/EamonTewell/status/1347226722752745474?s=20

5 Weaving the Longhouse "Four Rs" in LibGuides

Indigenous Teachings in Library Practice

Kayla Lar-Son, Karleen Delaurier-Lyle, and Sarah Dupont

Terminology

In Canada, the term *Aboriginal* is defined under Section 35 of the Constitution Act (1982) as including Indian (more respectfully referred to as status First Nations today), Métis, and Inuit peoples (Government of Canada, 1982). The authors, like many contemporary Canadians, use this word more broadly to include all First Nations (both status and non-status), Métis, and Inuit people. However, for the purpose of this article, In*digenous is* used instead of Ab*original,* although both can be used somewhat interchangeably when specifically referring to Canada's First Peoples. This choice reflects Xwi̱7xwa̱'s commitment to support the language used in the *Declaration on the Rights of Indigenous Peoples Act* (Queens Printer, 2019), which, with its passing in the Legislative Assembly, made British Columbia the first Canadian province to formally adopt the United Nations Declaration on Indigenous Peoples (UNDRIP) as law.

Indigenous Librarianship and Indigenous Librarians in a Canadian Context

Access for Indigenous peoples to information, library services, and information literacy has been historically overlooked by the library profession in the diverse aggregate of places we now call Canada. Library buildings and services in Indigenous communities were largely non-existent until the 1960s to 1970s and varied across the Canadian provinces and territories (Edwards, 2004). Arguably, these services are still lacking for the majority of these communities based on geographic locale, social and economic barriers, and the willingness of library systems to build relationships with local Indigenous communities in order to provide programs and services to the community. However, after the Truth and Reconciliation Commission (TRC) released their Calls to Action in 2015, many cultural heritage institutions, including libraries (although not formally called to action) and post-secondary institutions, have acknowledged their

DOI: 10.4324/9781003167174-6

commitments to reconciliation with Indigenous communities. This has generated an increase in reconciliation-driven programming, services, and policy changes.

In addition to the TRC, there has been a steady increase in Canadian librarians wanting to further engage Indigenous communities and change the way that they professionally practice librarianship to strengthen their commitment to bettering relationships and increasing services to Indigenous communities. Indigenous library and information studies (LIS) emerged as a distinct field of practice on an international scale in the late 20th century (Burns et al., 2009, p. 2). The key principles of Indigenous LIS are to provide culturally relevant services, collections, and programming. Indigenous librarianship aims to address the complex information requirements of Indigenous scholars, individuals, and communities that include a broad range of topics. Everything from the revitalization and maintenance of Indigenous cultures and languages, to self-governance, to rights and title claims, to stewardship of traditional territories and resources, to preservation of traditional knowledge systems, to municipal record keeping and standards; and a range of social, economic, and educational uses calls for layered services (Burns et al., 2009, p. 18). Above all, it applies Indigenous Ways of Knowing and Being into LIS practices, policies, and principles. It should be noted that Indigenous librarianship can be practiced by Indigenous librarians as well as non-Indigenous librarian allies.

Although non-Indigenous librarians can practice Indigenous LIS, it is distinctly the Indigenous librarians who are at the forefront of the profession. However, as of 2017, there were less than 25 Indigenous librarians with a Masters of Library and Information Studies (MLIS) currently working in libraries and archives across Canada (Lee, 2017, p. 176). Some issues identified as potential reasons for this give more insight into the problem. Lee (2017) suspects that barriers to entry and retention are the root cause of this disproportion. These barriers include:

- lack of financial resources to obtain a degree;
- lack of knowledge of librarianship as a profession;
- lack of advocacy for the profession;
- the emotions factor;
- pay differences; and
- the issue of self-identification (p. 180).

University of British Columbia (UBC) Libraries, at a large Canadian academic institution, is privileged to have four Indigenous academic librarians and one Indigenous support staff working full time. There are also Indigenous individuals with an MLIS degree working in other departments and cultural heritage institutions at UBC, such as the Museum of Anthropology and the Indian Residential School History & Dialogue

Centre. Part of the draw to UBC Libraries for Indigenous librarians is the support, comradery, stable employment, and career mentorship they receive through Xwi7xwa Library.

Xwi7xwa Library

Xwi7xwa Library is the first and only Indigenous branch of an academic library at a post-secondary institution in Canada. Built in 1993, its history is woven tightly to that of the First Nations Longhouse, which was built at the same time. Together, the UBC First Nations Longhouse and Xwi7xwa make up the First Nations House of Learning (FNHL). The Elders who envisioned the Longhouse felt strongly that a First Nations Library was needed in close proximity for the students. They succeeded in finding a principal donor to fund this building: Mr. William Bellman. Xwi7xwa is named after him, as he was gifted the name Xwi7xwa by Squamish Elder and Chief, Koot-la-cha, at the opening ceremony for the Longhouse and the Library. The Xwi7xwa Library collection consists almost exclusively of Indigenous-created materials. It uses its own version of the Brian Deer Classification system and unique subject headings that take into account Indigenous worldviews (Xwi7xwa Library, 2021c). Additionally, Xwi7xwa's building is designed after structures built by Interior Salish nations. In the Chinook Jargon, this structure is called a *Kekuli;* in English, it is called a pit house; and in 7ˋ *Ucwalmicwts* (Lil'wat nation), it is called a *S7ístken* (Xwi7xwa Library, 2021a).

The Longhouse and Xwi7xwa share a logo created by Tsimshian artist, Glen Wood, that consists of a human face surrounded by two ravens, which also form the frame of a longhouse. The face represents First Nations people and the house design represents the university (Doyle et al., 2015, p. 101). The logo represents Raven transforming the university to reflect First Nations cultures, Knowledges, and worldviews; linking the university to First Nations and other Indigenous communities. It evokes a two-dimensional vision of Indigenization within the academy: a focus on Indigenous values and Knowledges, and a commitment to institutional and social change. These dual aspects are manifested at the Xwi7xwa Library through its professional practice and scholarship (Doyle et al., 2015, p. 101).

The Four Rs of the UBC Longhouse

As Indigenous librarians, we cannot separate our worldview from our professional practices. These worldviews govern how we interact with all of our relations, hold ourselves accountable to the community, and practice our own self-care. As Xwi7xwa library is located on the unceded territories of the *xʷməθkʷəy̓əm* (Musqueam), *Sḵwx̱wú7mesh* (Squamish), and *Selíl̓witulh* (Tsleil-Waututh) Nations, in what is now known as Vancouver, and acknowledging our close relationship with the Longhouse, we incorporate the Four Rs of the Longhouse into our library professional practice and personal worldview.

The late Elder Tsimilano often invited people to "form a circle and join hands in prayer. In joining hands, hold your left palm upward to reach back to grasp the teachings of the Ancestors. Hold your right palm downward to pass these teachings on to the younger generation. In this way, the teachings of the ancestors continue and the circle of human understanding and caring grows stronger" (UBC, 2019). The Four R teachings of *respect, relationships, responsibility, and reverence* allow for the continued strengthening of the circle of understanding and growth for both the Longhouse and Xwi7xwa library (UBC, 2019) through the recognition of Indigenous worldviews. These allow us to see the whole person as interconnected to land and in relationship to others.

Respect forms the foundation for other values. *Respect* begins with self and then ripples out to embrace family, community, nations, the natural world, and the creator. This teaching is honored by:

- acknowledging the land and the Coast Salish and Musqueam peoples of the land;
- maintaining a safe, healthy, inclusive environment free of alcohol and drugs, discrimination, and harassment;
- caring for our home and the surrounding environment; and
- being sensitive to the needs of other users (UBC, 2019).

Relationships speaks to the connection to all creation and the Creator. The teaching of "all my relations" is honored by:

- valuing the gifts and teachings which come to us through our relations and with those of different ages, ancestry, color, family, status, marital status, physical or mental disability, political belief, place of origin, race, religion, sex, sexual orientation, and unrelated criminal conviction;
- interacting with discretion;
- considering the needs of Elders and children in our actions and activities; and
- welcoming visitors with honor and consideration (UBC, 2019).

Responsibility is when we understand what enhances wellbeing and what diminishes it, and we take responsibility for strengthening it. This teaching is honored by:

- modeling and sharing protocol with others;
- caring for ourselves, others, the Longhouse, and the environment;
- serving as witnesses in the unfolding life of the Longhouse; and
- using resources appropriately (UBC, 2019).

Reverence is the meeting of respect and the sacred. This teaching is honored by:

- serving others for the benefit of all our relations;
- developing our own gifts and facilitating that development in others;
- being grateful for our lives and the lives of all in our circle of relations; and
- being respectful of the spiritual realm and its place in learning (UBC, 2019).

Interpretations of the Four Rs in a Post-Secondary Context

In this paper, we focus on how we connect the UBC Longhouse Four Rs to the X̱wi7x̱wa library's practices, services, and LibGuides; however, it is important to acknowledge other interpretations of the Four Rs in a post-secondary context. Kirkness and Barnhardt (1991) were the first to introduce the Four Rs into a post-secondary context. The Four Rs were outlined so that post-secondary institutions could better support Indigenous students entering university in a way that reflected their own worldviews. For Kirkness and Barnhardt (1991), the Four Rs include respect, relevance, reciprocity, and responsibility (p. 6). *Respect* is understood as respect for First Nations cultural identity; this includes respect for cultural differences and worldviews (Kirkness & Barnhardt, 1991, pp. 7–8).

For Kirkness and Barnhardt, *Relevance* called on post-secondary institutions to legitimize Indigenous Knowledges and foster ways to incorporate them into academia (Kirkness & Barnhardt, 1991, p. 8). This had to be, and still needs to be, done in a way that acknowledges Indigenous Knowledge protocols. Additionally, Kirkness and Barnhardt call on post-secondary institutions to examine their policies, practices, and protocols to ensure that they are relevant to Indigenous communities (p. 9). *Reciprocity* within an Indigenous worldview is highly valued; teaching and learning are and should be reciprocal processes. Reciprocity can be achieved when faculty members make an effort to understand a student's cultural background and the student is able to access the inner-workings of the culture and institution to which they are being introduced (p. 10). *Responsibility* through participation is the understanding that for post-secondary institutions, they have a responsibility to Indigenous students and communities to create a welcoming environment for Indigenous students (p. 10), and to partner with Indigenous communities to maintain, develop, and ensure the future of Indigenous programs and services (p. 13).

The Indigenous Strategic Plan (ISP) was officially introduced to the larger UBC community and celebrated in September of 2020. It consists of 8 goals and 43 actions. Consultation for the ISP was conducted across both UBC campuses: UBC Vancouver and UBC Okanagan, and was created with input from students, faculty and staff, both Indigenous and non. The ISP is UBC's response to the United Nations Declaration on the Rights of Indigenous Peoples (UNDRIP) and the National Inquiry for Missing and Murdered Indigenous Women and Girls. The ISP is also one of UBC's responses to the TRC's Calls to Action (UBC, 2021). Within the ISP, the Four Rs are acknowledged in the document's section on engagement, specifically in regards to the engagement process pertaining to research with Indigenous communities. Like the Longhouse's teachings, the ISP uses the same Four R values of *respect, relationship, responsibility, and reverence* as a guide in how to engage with Indigenous communities and research (UBC, 2020, p. 15).

BC Campus is an organization whose primary focus is to support post-secondary institutions of British Columbia as they adopt, adapt, and evolve their teaching and learning practices to create a better experience for Indigenous students (BC Campus, 2021). In their open educational resource (OER) *Pulling Together: A Guide for Front-Line Staff, Student Services, and Advisors* (Cull et al., 2018), BC Campus outlines their understanding of the Four Rs within a post-secondary context that aims to ensure that post-secondary institutions become accessible, inclusive, safe, and successful places for Indigenous students (Caldwell, 2020). The main difference between this interpretation, the Four Rs as outlined by the Longhouse and Kirkness and Barnhardt (1991), and the ISP is that *reverence* is replaced by *relevance*. The following is how the Four Rs are interpreted in *Pulling Together:*

Respect encompasses an understanding of and practicing community protocols, honors Indigenous Knowledges and Ways of Being, and considers in a reflective and non-judgmental way what is being seen and heard (Cull et al., 2018, p. 26).

Responsibility is inclusive of students, the institution, and Indigenous communities; it also recognizes one's own connections to various communities. It continually seeks to develop and sustain credible relationships with Indigenous communities. It is important to be seen in the community as both a supporter and a representative of the institution. *Responsibility* means understanding the potential impact of one's motives and intentions on oneself and the community. It honors that the integrity of Indigenous people and Indigenous communities must not be undermined or disrespected when working with Indigenous people (Cull et al., 2018, pp. 26–27).

Relevance ensures that curricula, services, and programs are responsive to the needs identified by Indigenous students and communities. It involves Indigenous communities in the designing of academic curricula and student services across the institution to ensure Indigenous Knowledge is valued and that the curricula have culturally appropriate outcomes and assessments. It centers meaningful and sustainable community engagement (Cull et al., 2018, p. 27).

Reciprocity shares knowledge throughout the entire educational process. Staff create interdepartmental learning and succession planning between colleagues to ensure practices and knowledge are continued. Shared learning embodies the principle of reciprocity. This means Indigenous and non-Indigenous people are both learning in process together. Within an educational setting, this may mean staff to student, student to student, or faculty to staff; each of these relationships honors the knowledge and gifts that each person brings to the classroom, workplace, and institution. The result of this is that all who are involved within the institution, including the broader Indigenous communities, gain experience in sharing knowledge in a respectful way. All participants are viewed as students and teachers in the process (Cull et al., 2018, p. 27).

LibGuides and Social Responsibility

LibGuides are content management systems that are used by thousands of libraries nationally and internationally that allow for the sharing of carefully curated content and organize the information based on subject or class (Springshare, 2020). LibGuides that specifically focus on social justice content are a fairly new development in library practice; however, libraries do not operate outside of society. By this, we mean *-isms* and *-phobias* are inherent in the people who work within them, as well as in the very structures of our organizations (Hodge, 2020). Therefore, LibGuides can act as a library tool to allow individuals to engage with difficult subjects, unlearn what they have previously been taught, and unpack unconscious biases. As identified in Kostelecky (2018), libraries can demonstrate support for diverse communities when they reframe the purpose of LibGuides in a way that shares content generated in communities, thus acknowledging "their commitment to truly being engaged in creating a democratic society via information sharing and acknowledging community-created information and community expertise" (p. 11). Libraries can also use LibGuides as a way of highlighting diverse voices and perspectives and challenge the academic understanding of who is considered an expert (Kostelecky, 2018, p. 12).

Within a Canadian context, there are few social justice LibGuides that are dedicated to a specific movement. LibGuides that do focus more on the broader topic of social justice, such as Capilano University's *Intersectionality & Social Justice* LibGuide, can be a living resource on ageism, anti-racism, inclusive teaching, Indigenous activism, intersectionality, neurodiversity and ability, queer issues, sizeism, socio-economic status, and women and gender. Each of these topics has a dedicated tab within the guide (Capilano University, 2021). These broader guides are generally created to support specific research needs of that institution's faculty and students.

Several Canadian universities have created LibGuides to support Indigenous studies as a discipline and to support larger university decolonization efforts. In general, content in Indigenous focused LibGuides consists of resources that support Indigenous studies courses, such as how to find materials, Indigenous perspectives on research, and information on Indigenous Knowledges. Canadian academic library LibGuides that pertain to specific Indigenous social movements are rare; however, content on movements, such as Idle No More (McGill University, 2020; University of Winnipeg, 2021), and more recently, *Unist'ot'en/Wet'suwet'en* (Brandon University, 2021; UBCO Libraries, 2021; University of Victoria, 2020) can be found embedded within guides for the disciplines of Indigenous studies, LIS, and law and policy classes.

It is important to acknowledge that Indigenous LibGuides in Canada have been curated by both Indigenous and non-Indigenous librarians. Indigenous librarian-authored LibGuides can act as a space in which it is possible for Indigenous librarians to express perspectives, world views, and lived experiences in scholarly conversation. Simultaneously, Indigenous librarians can be recognized as Indigenous experts themselves, rather than outsiders who write about Indigenous communities, Indigenous social issues, and participate in Indigenous LIS without having lived experience to inform the content (Kostelecky, 2018). Additionally, LibGuides that are created by Indigenous librarians can act as a form of their own personal accountability to Indigenous communities to share information in a way that is accessible to their members, while at the same time, adhere to any specific Indigenous Knowledge-sharing protocols that the community may identify. An example of that would be not sharing sensitive community or community-owned Knowledge to a non-community member, or to inappropriate members within the community.

X̱wi7x̱wa Library LibGuides

As of April 2021, X̱wi7x̱wa library has twenty published LibGuides available through the Research Guides Portal (Xwi7xwa Library, 2021j) (See Figure 5.1) Eleven additional guides, authored by other UBC branches, are included at the bottom of the portal due to their relevance in Indigenous subject areas, and of these, X̱wi7x̱wa Librarians have contributed to some. X̱wi7x̱wa LibGuides are largely created based on topics or subject areas frequently inquired about by patrons, as well as current local and global events related to Indigenous topics of interest. While the branch's patron base is broad in scope (from local Indigenous community members to researchers across the globe), the focal point of this work is with the FNHL students, staff, and faculty in mind with a ripple effect outward. This is not to say X̱wi7x̱wa's efforts toward resourcing and supporting non-FNHL community members is not a priority; rather, it is that the branch's origin is rooted here and the work should first start at home. For the most part, X̱wi7x̱wa LibGuides focus on a topic or subject area. The two exceptions to this are the Indigenous Education – NITEP (Xwi7xwa Library, 2021b) guide, which focuses on providing access and bibliographic instruction to a specific library user group, and the Distance Research Guide (Xwi7xwa Library, 2021i), which focuses on research with a completely virtual environment in mind. Overall, X̱wi7x̱wa's LibGuides are intended to support research on

Xwi7xwa Library - Distance Research Guide

First Nations & Indigenous Studies	Indigenous Education K-12
Aboriginal Languages	Indigenous Education - NITEP
Aboriginal Maps and Mapping	Indigenous Librarianship
Aboriginal Treaties	Indigenous New Media
Aboriginal Films and Filmmakers	Indigenous Research Methodology
Indian Residential Schools in Canada	Métis Studies
Indigenous Publishers, Distributors & News Media	Missing and Murdered Indigenous Women & Girls
Indigenous Children's Literature	Musqueam Research Guide
Two-Spirit and Indigiqueer Studies	Indigenous Land Based Activism
Indigenous Music & Dance	Decolonization & Anti-Racism

Figure 5.1 X̱wi7x̱wa Library Research Guide Portal

a given subject or topic that responsibly surfaces information sources for Indigenous students, staff, faculty, and all other patrons.

X̱wi7x̱wa LibGuides: Incorporating Longhouse Teachings

Elder Tsimilano's *Hands Back, Hands Forward* teaching asks us to extend our left palm upward, look back, and reflect on our own origin as a branch. As part of the FNHL community, the first phase of understanding patron needs happens through the relationship(s) X̱wi7x̱wa has with its own community. These spaces offer support for Indigenous students, staff, and faculty first and foremost. The spaces have also been a meeting place for visiting family, friends, Elders, and non-Indigenous researchers, both within and outside of UBC. For this reason, the creation of LibGuides starts with FNHL students and extends outward accordingly.

Relationship: LibGuides are available to anyone with an internet connection and a device to access it. LibGuide users are therefore diverse in perspectives, beliefs, educational backgrounds, understandings of Indigenous studies, and personal identity/lived experiences of the world. The act of developing the X̱wi7x̱wa LibGuides, therefore, must anticipate *all our relations.* As LibGuides play a role in bridging information to patrons and vice-versa, a great deal of care is taken when deciding what information is put forward and how it is presented. For example, a warning and self-care disclaimer is added to topics that relate to systemic and colonial violence. X̲wi7x̲wa LibGuide authors consider how our immediate community audiences may have personal relationships to various information sources and topics. Specifically, some patrons may have personal ties and relationships to Missing & Murdered Indigenous Women, Girls, & Two-Spirit (MMIWG2S). Therefore, our MMIWG2S LibGuide (X̲wi7x̲wa Library, 2021e) contains both disclaimers and resources for rematriation, healing, empowerment, and resiliency, to support those who are looking at the guide for research and/or personal reasons. X̲wi7x̲wa LibGuides evoke the Longhouse teaching of *relationship* as we welcome all patrons and the perspectives and experiences they bring. X̲wi7x̲wa works with discretion to ensure patrons are respected in their information seeking needs. By following this teaching, the branch actively maintains existing, and builds new, relationships (see Figure 5.2).

Respect: As previously mentioned, LibGuides (as one library resource) are created with a broad patron scope in mind, but prioritize localized needs. One of the main ways X̲wi7x̲wa continually understands the teaching of respect is by honoring our responsibilities to our host nation Musqueam and their Coast Salish neighbors: Squamish and Tsleil-Waututh (MST). In our professional practice as information professionals, this means ensuring we share information with care. One expectation for us is to respectfully share information Indigenous nations have made publicly available and want to share with the world at large.

Figure 5.2 MMIWG2S LibGuide

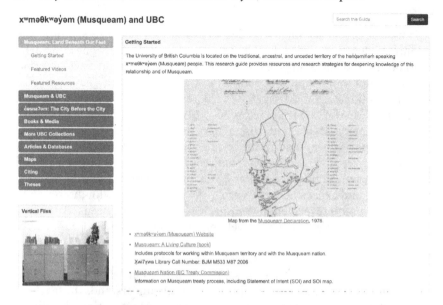

Figure 5.3 xʷməθkʷəy̓əm (Musqueam) and UBC LibGuide

The xʷməθkʷəy̓əm (Musqueam) & UBC LibGuide (Xwi7xwa Library, 2021g) bring forth resources published and publicly available that have been created in *a good way* (with respect to, in collaboration with, or from the community itself), rather than prioritizing historical perspectives by authors writing *about* Indigenous people. It highlights key resources about the relationship between UBC, as an occupier of traditional Musqueam lands, and Musqueam, the host nation. Through the teaching of respect, X̱wi7x̱wa LibGuides ensure naming, identity, and general information about a specific community/nation is current and more accurately describes a people *on* and *with* their own terms. By respecting physical, online, and land-based spaces, X̱wi7x̱wa creates safer online resources for diverse users (see Figure 5.3).

Responsibility: Responsibility serves as a constant reminder of good practice as X̱wi7x̱wa LibGuides surface resources on specific topics and shares this information with the world at large. As an example, the Two-Spirit & Indigiqueer LibGuide (Xwi7xwa Library, 2021h) was created after a pattern of reference questions led to the realization that Two-Spirit and Indigiqueer perspectives and representations were not easily findable within the X̱wi7x̱wa collection. This issue is not unique to X̱wi7x̱wa; it is replicated in many other locales and resources, such as reports, library collections, archives, organizations, institutions, policies, and more (see Figure 5.4).

While upholding key resources and search strategies, the aforementioned LibGuide also seeks to reflect Two-Spirit and Indigiqueer perspectives at local and national levels. The LibGuide highlights local efforts from all

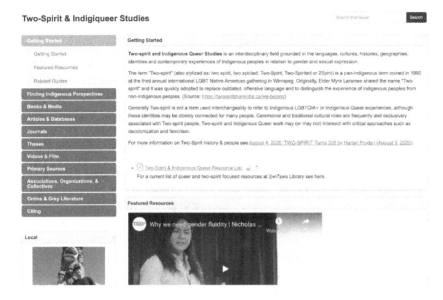

Figure 5.4 Two-Spirit & Indigiqueer LibGuide

MST territories, UBC, and within local Vancouver programs for urban dwelling people. Given that the guide's origin lies in either a lack of, or difficulty in finding, Two-Spirit and Indigiqueer representation/perspectives, it becomes the LibGuides' responsibility to fill the gap by connecting patrons with information on this 2S topic. This responsibility is carried out in other LibGuides as well. For example, the MMIWG2S LibGuide purposefully highlights these perspectives in the National Action Plan tab (Xwi7xwa Library, 2021f), since the original MMIWG2S report, too, upheld a lack of Two-Spirit and Indigiqueer representations.

Reverence: The Longhouse teaching of reverence asks us to recognize and embed our gifts in our work: "what is (y)our role?." X̱wi7x̱wa is an information hub that connects patrons and information and it acts as an information conduit. Information professionals tasked with the creation of LibGuides understand that reverence asks us to understand all of the Longhouse teachings enmeshed into deliverables (in this case, the LibGuides themselves). These resources are then shared with patrons in order to support and uphold their individual and collective work. As Indigenous information professionals, the goals of our work are tied to community, national, and international pursuits of Indigenous goals. Some examples include, but are not limited to: decolonization, sovereignty, language and cultural revitalization, education, and politics. An understanding of information creation, maintenance, care, release, and sharing is a gift and strength of Indigenous librarians; reverence asks how this gift upholds those we work for and with.

Reverence also serves as a reminder for how we (in)directly impact one another as Indigenous people.

With this teaching in hand, X̱wi7x̱wa is given a touchstone on how to mediate what is shared based on where questions come from and how the information we connect patrons with will impact Indigenous people as a whole. As an example, the Indigenous Land Based Activism LibGuide (X̱wi7x̱wa Library, 2021d) was created to support the (often repeated) research questions related to pipelines, land/water-based protection, and Indigenous movements/demonstrations in response to Canadian/US resource extraction. This LibGuide surfaces Indigenous perspectives and concepts related to land-based activism and has even supported FNHL events, such as the Wet'suwet'en Virtual Teach-In (University of British Columbia Learning Circle, 2020). X̱wi7x̱wa responsibly shared this LibGuide by avoiding the use of specific social media hashtags being utilized by land and water protectors. Since the use of hashtags via social media channels was one way for protectors to communicate current events, the branch used broader hashtags when sharing these LibGuides with patrons, rather than the specific ones being used by the activists.

Conclusion

X̱wi7x̱wa's LibGuides are unique in that their creators are asked to recognize how the collection and distribution of resources will impact current and future work. Elder Tsimilano's teaching asks us to extend our right palm downward, reminding us of our impact on our relations (with special attentive efforts to our FNHL community and host nation). X̱wi7x̱wa LibGuides are not outside the social and political movements and world we are currently living and they uphold resources intended for action. They are created based on repeated research questions on important topics that interest and impact Indigenous people, and they carry a responsibility for making a positive impact. We consistently rely on and turn to our Longhouse teachings in fulfilling this responsibility. All the librarians at the X̱wi7x̱wa Library are Indigenous-identifying individuals whose existence as Indigenous peoples and information professionals is inherently political; therefore, our positions and practices cannot be neutral. We cannot remain neutral in discussions of social justice and Indigenous rights, as we are accountable to Indigenous communities, and acknowledge all our relations. Due to our positionalities, our work outputs, including the LibGuides we write, are based on a recognized need for collected information on social justice movements and other activism regarding Indigenous issues, and cannot claim to be neutral. The positionality and motive of the researcher is something we try to take into account as we author these guides as well. Are they using these guides for research that will, ultimately, help Indigenous peoples and/or themselves along their personal journey of reconciliation? Or does the potential exist that the works we bring together and publish in the guides could be misconstrued and somehow weaponized against Indigenous peoples, with or without this intent? While we ultimately have little control over this, we have to think carefully about our responsibilities to Indigenous communities with the work we do.

This leads us to ask you, our colleagues, to consider carefully what the purpose of your LibGuide is. Is it to use the voice this platform gives to librarians to inform more broadly about an issue, or is it rather just to provide links to resources? We hope this chapter has inspired you to do some of the hard work required to Indigenize your LibGuides, in every subject area you represent, as Indigenous Knowledges are not siloed into western-defined disciplines. Using the framework of the Four Rs, this important work can be achieved thoughtfully by both Indigenous and non-Indigenous authors.

Acknowledgments

Xwi7xwa would like to both acknowledge and thank our former student librarians, Bronte Burnette-Chiang and Isabel Krupp; and current student librarians Bronwen McKie, Tamara Lee, Kajola Morewood, and Rio Picollo for their contributions to Xwi7xwa LibGuides. We also acknowledge former Xwi7xwa librarian Kim Lawson for her prior work in developing and maintaining some of our earlier LibGuides. Thank you to the other amazing Xwi7xwa team members, Tamis Cochrane and Eleanore Wellwood, for your constant support and guidance. Lastly, we would like to also acknowledge all the other past, present, and future Indigenous librarians who have and will continue to advocate for transformative change in indigenizing cultural heritage institutions. In solidarity: hiy hiy, marsee, meegwetch, and hay č xʷ q̓ ə.

References

BC Campus. (2021). *About Us*, BC Campus. https://bccampus.ca/about-us/.

Brandon University. (2021). *Indigenous resources – background, policy, analysis: Unist'ot'en/Wet'suwet'en*, Brandon University. https://libguides.brandonu.ca/indigenous/wet.

Burns, K., Doyle, A. M., Joseph, G., & Krebs, A. (2009). Indigenous librarianship. In M. J. Bates, & M. N. Maack (Eds.), *Encyclopedia of library and information sciences* (3rd ed.). Taylor & Francis.

Caldwell, J. (2020). *Indigenization guide: Indigenous ways of knowing and being*, BC Campus. https://bccampus.ca/2020/11/23/indigenization-guide-indigenous-ways-of-knowing-and-being/.

Capilano University (2021). Intersectinallity & Social Justice Libguide, https://libguides.capilanou.ca/social_justice

Cull, I., Hancock, R. L. A., McKeown, S., Pidgeon, M., & Vedan, A. (2018). *Pulling together: A guide for front-line staff, student services, and advisors*. BC campus. Retrieved from https://opentextbc.ca/indigenizationfrontlineworkers/.

Doyle, A. M., Lawson, K., & Dupont, S. (2015). Indigenization of knowledge organization at the Xwi7xwa library. *Journal of Library and Information Studies, 13*(2), 107–134. doi: 10.6182/jlis.2015.13(2).107.

Edwards, B. (2004). *Paper talk: A history of libraries, print culture, and aboriginal peoples in Canada Before 1960.* Scarecrow Press.

Government of Canada. (1982). *Canadian Constitution Act Part 2, Section* 35 *(2).* https://caid.ca/ConstAct010208.pdf.

Hodge, T. (2020). *Using LibGuides to support racial justice & create inclusive communities,* Springshare Buzz. https://buzz.springshare.com/springynews/news-49/libguides-tricks?preview=f765068afa3d2ae2aaea74a6f422af87#s-lg-box-24462157.

Kirkness, V., & Barnhardt, R. (1991). First nations and higher education: The four R's – respect, relevance, reciprocity, responsibility. *Journal of American Indian Education, 30*(3), 1–15. Retrieved April 30, 2021, from http://www.jstor.org/stable/24397980.

Kostelecky, S. R. (2018). Sharing community created content in support of social justice: The Dakota Access Pipeline LibGuide. *Journal of Librarianship & Scholarly Communication, 6*, 1–16. doi: 10.7710/2162-3309.2234.

Lee, D. (2017). Discussion section: Indigenous librarians: Knowledge keepers in the 21st century. *Canadian Journal of Native Studies, 37*(1), 175–199. doi: 10.33137/cjal-rcbu.v5.29922.

McGill University. (2020). *Group 3: Introduction: Defining Decolonization,* McGill School of Library and Information Studies. https://mcgill-lis.libguides.com/c.php?g=719698&p=5143181.

Queens Printer. (2019). *Bill 41 – 2019: Declaration on the Rights of Indigenous Peoples.* Legislative Assembly of British Columbia. https://www.leg.bc.ca/parliamentary-business/legislation-debates-proceedings/41st-parliament/4th-session/bills/first-reading/gov41-1/.

Springshare. (2020). LibGuides, Springshare. https://springshare.com/libguides/.

UBCO Libraries. (2021). *WET 219 – applied water law,* Okanagan Library. https://libguides.okanagan.bc.ca/c.php?g=708598&p=5098969.

University of British Columbia. (2019). *Longhouse Teachings,* Indigenous Portal. https://indigenous.ubc.ca/longhouse/longhouse-teachings/.

University of British Columbia. (2020). *UBC Indigenous Strategic Plan.* https://aboriginal-2018.sites.olt.ubc.ca/files/2020/09/UBC.ISP_C2V13.1_Spreads_Sept1.pdf.

University of British Columbia. (2021). *Indigenous Strategic Plan,* Indigenous Portal, https://indigenous.ubc.ca/indigenous-engagement/indigenous-strategic-plan/.

University of British Columbia Learning Circle. (2020). *April 9th, 2020 – Wet'suwet'en Virtual Teach-In,* Faculty of Medicine Learning Circle/Centre for Excellence in Indigenous Health. https://learningcircle.ubc.ca/2020/03/26/wetsuweten-learning/.

University of Victoria. (2020). *Gitxsan and Indigenous Property Law,* Transsystemic Property Law – LAW 107I. https://libguides.uvic.ca/c.php?g=706189&p=5025084.

University of Winnipeg. (2021). *Race, Racialization and Racism,* University of Winnipeg Libraries. https://libguides.uwinnipeg.ca/c.php?g=370387&p=3913489.

Xwi7xwa Library. (2021a). How do you pronounce the name of the X̱wi7x̱wa Library? What does it mean? About Xwi7xwa Library. https://xwi7xwa.library.ubc.ca/about/.

Xwi7xwa Library. (2021b). *Indigenous Education – NITEP,* Xwi7xwa Library. https://guides.library.ubc.ca/nitep.

Xwi7xwa Library. (2021c). *Indigenous Knowledge Organization*, Xwi7xwa Library. https://xwi7xwa.library.ubc.ca/collections/indigenous-knowledge-organization/

Xwi7xwa Library. (2021d). *Indigenous Land Based Activism*, Xwi7xwa Library. https://guides.library.ubc.ca/landbasedactivism/home.

Xwi7xwa Library. (2021e). *Missing and Murdered Indigenous Women, Girls, & Two-Spirit (MMIWG2S)*, Xwi7xwa Library. https://guides.library.ubc.ca/mmiwg.

Xwi7xwa Library. (2021f). *MMIWG Inquiry*, Missing and Murdered Indigenous Women, Girls, & Two-Spirit (MMIWG2S). https://guides.library.ubc.ca/mmiwg/nationalinquiry.

Xwi7xwa Library. (2021g). *xʷməθkʷəy̓əm (Musqueam) and UBC*, Xwi7xwa Library. https://guides.library.ubc.ca/Musqueam.

Xwi7xwa Library. (2021h). *Two-Spirit and Indigiqueer Studies*, Xwi7xwa Library. https://guides.library.ubc.ca/twospiritandindigenousqueerstudies.

Xwi7xwa Library. (2021i). *Xwi7xwa – Distance Learning*, Xwi7xwa Library. https://guides.library.ubc.ca/distance-research-xwi7xwa.

Xwi7xwa Library. (2021j). *Xwi7xwa Research Guides: Home*, Xwi7xwa Library. https://guides.library.ubc.ca/xwi7xwaresearchguide.

6 Bringing Diverse Library Exhibitions and Events to life

Essraa Nawar

Introduction

Education at Chapman is about more than academics and part of our mission is to educate students to be Global Citizens who not only understand the complexities of their local and regional communities but also learn how to engage beyond that parameter. I have the honor of serving as the Chair of the Arts, Exhibits and Events committee here at the library. The committee works collaboratively to bring diverse and rich programming to life. We choose programs that complement and enhance the curriculum, study, and research interests at Chapman University. Putting together these exhibits and programs takes a lot of brainstorming and exchange of ideas between the members of the committee. In fact, our efforts were recently recognized by a Diversity and Talent Management Diversity, Equity, and Inclusion (DEI) Initiatives award through the Council for Advancement & Support of Education (CASE) (Karas, R. 2021).

Commitment to Diversity and Social Justice

The Leatherby Libraries at Chapman University values and understands the importance of diversity, and to demonstrate that value, works diligently on creating programming and exhibits that emphasize this value in myriad ways (Ross & Nawar, 2021). The Leatherby Libraries offers activities throughout the academic year that complement and enhance the curriculum, study, and research interests at Chapman University. The library's Arts, Exhibits and Events Committee collaborates with other departments on campus, other library groups, library friends, and university donors, trustees, and senior administrators and the wider community to bring authentic and diverse exhibitions and their accompanying programming to life. Such collaborations and exhibitions have resulted in many educational opportunities for the students, faculty, staff, and the larger community. They also helped in breaking stereotypes, achieving national recognition, media attention, partnerships, sponsorships, and gifts to either the library or the University.

DOI: 10.4324/9781003167174-7

Chapman University Statement on Diversity & Inclusion

Chapman University is deeply committed to enriching diversity and inclusion to cultivate a welcoming campus climate for all members of the community. The University strives to develop meaningful outreach programs and partnerships with our diverse local communities. The university believed that an inclusive learning environment facilitates complex, critical, and creative thinking and that differences in identities, values, beliefs, and perspectives are fundamental to a comprehensive education. The term diversity at Chapman implies a respect for all and an understanding of individual differences including race, color, religion, sex, gender identity, gender expression, pregnancy, national origin, ancestry, citizenship status, age, marital status, physical disability, mental disability, medical condition, sexual orientation, military or veteran status, genetic information, and any other characteristic protected by applicable state or federal law so that all members of the community are treated at all times with dignity and respect.

The Role of the Libraries

The Leatherby Libraries play an integral role in the university's teaching, learning, and research. The library's vision and mission statements enforce the library's increasing leadership role in the life and culture of the campus and community and are committed to the mission of global education and embrace the call for diversity. Through its arts, exhibits, and event committee, the library offers yearly unique and diverse programs that entices conversations and creates a language of understanding and dialogue in the University's Community. The following few case studies/examples showcase how the library not only capitalizes on current campus, national and international events but also uses their own staffs' and students' diverse skills, background, and connections to bring these programs to life.

Programs like Empowering Muslim women, Egypt the Revolution Continues, Black History Month, A portrait of a people: a Jewish exhibition, Sikh cultural exhibitions, Pride Month displays, Interfaith exhibits and recently A Country called Syria (and much more) not only enhances the educational experience for the students and the surrounding community but help them discover, explore, and visualize unknown parts of the world and create a culture of acceptance and understanding.

The Art, Exhibits, and Events Committee (AEEC)

In alignment with the vision of the Leatherby Libraries to be a preeminent portal to the world's knowledge, an intellectual and cultural center of campus, and a distinguished resource for teaching, learning, and scholarship at Chapman University. The Leatherby Libraries established a committee dedicated to bringing exhibitions, and events to life. This committee is a dedicated group of 10 to 12 library staff and librarians who volunteer their time, talent, and energy to create innovative and educational programming to engage the students and the faculty beyond the walls of the classroom. Everybody is welcome to participate but we must include a member or two from the circulation staff for communication linkages, so they are aware of what is going on and can advise on hours of operations (adjusting opening/closing hours) and any maintenance and facility needs. The committee consists of:

- Term: Two years, committee letters (Show committee letters)
- Two co-chairs (The Dean and the Development Librarian).
- Meeting twice a month for one hour each time.
- Regular communication by email for updates and voting on time-sensitive matters.
- Minutes, agendas, photos, and committee business are kept/organized in the library's shared folder for all Library Staff and Administrators to monitor.
- The AEEC's budget is part of the library's operating budget but for the past few years most of the library programming has been sponsored by donors or other departments on campus. This has led to extra funds available for professional development and other library needs.

Why the Arts, Exhibits, and Events Committee?

- Assures the offering of programming, displays, and exhibits throughout the year.
- Ensures the diversity of programs and exhibits displays through the participation of different members of the staff and librarians in the committee and ensuring the representation of a wide variety of perspectives, speakers and collections highlighted.
- Assures that there are no conflicts and redundancy with events and programming.
- Communicates library events and programs on a regular basis to library staff members and other constituents such as the strategic marketing and communications office to ensure branding along with the public relations office for publicity purposes and to ensure that the library's events and exhibits get covered in campus emails and magazines.
- Ensures the appropriate staffing for these events.
- Complements and enhances the curriculum, study, and research interests at the University.
- Tracks events, exhibitions, and displays throughout the year for budget, reporting, and historical archiving purposes.

Sikh Initiatives at Chapman University

The Leatherby Libraries enjoys a rich partnership with several Sikh organizations in Orange County since 2012. The project is a collaborative partnership between the Leatherby Libraries and Sikhlens founder Bicky Singh, Chapman University Board of Governors member, and was established in 2012 to promote a variety of Sikh Initiatives across campus(Karas, R. n.d.b). This partnership has provided an avenue to increase the understanding of Sikh values in order to raise awareness of the impact on Sikh culture both on campus and around the world. Since this collaborative partnership was formed eight years ago, Sikh initiatives have focused on telling the story of Sikh religion and culture through exhibits, lectures, and interfaith programs. This collaborative partnership provides a way for the university to continue its commitment to enriching diversity and inclusion and supports its mission of nurturing students to become global citizens. In November 2016, the Leatherby Libraries celebrated part of that partnership, through the generous help of donor Gurvendra Suri, with the opening of the Sikhs and Sikhism in America Group Study Room, located on the second floor of the Leatherby Libraries in Room 208.

Curated by Leatherby Libraries former Dean Charlene Baldwin, Development Coordinator and Librarian Essraa Nawar, and Curator Keerat Bajaj, the room contains a wealth of information and objects that teach students about the Sikh faith and community. Included in this story room are portraits on the wall of famous and notable Sikh Americans, maps and data about Sikh temples, or gurdwaras, in the United States and Orange County (including the temple closest to campus), turbans (Turban Display, 2014), and a stunning model of the Golden Temple, or Harmandir Sahib, of Amritsar, Punjab, India (see Figure 6.1). In addition, the walls of the room bear sayings from the Sikh faith, written in Punjabi script, transliterated Latin alphabet, and a translation into English (see Figure 6.1). The Sikhs and Sikhism in America Group Study Room offer Chapman University students a place where they can surround themselves with key images, objects, and text from a culture they might not otherwise be exposed to.

As a result of the overwhelming success of these library initiatives, Sikhlens has expanded their collaborative efforts and has worked with Chapman University's Dodge College of Film and Media Arts to create a program that enabled film students to travel abroad to immerse themselves in the Sikh culture. Sikhlens has also partnered with the university to curate various events and experiences to enrich the lives of both students and the local/regional community. Opportunities included the creation of a travel course to India to learn about the Sikh culture and heritage, a series of Sikh music and dance performances at the new Musco Center for the Arts, an annual dinner for Chapman's 200+ international students,

Figure 6.1 Sikhs and Sikhism in America Story Room

a yearly Vaisakhi (Sikh New Year) celebration at the Fish Interfaith Center, and an annual Sikh art exhibit displayed at Chapman's Leatherby Libraries (see Figure 6.2). This collaborative partnership provides a way for the university to continue its commitment to enriching diversity and inclusion and supports its mission of nurturing students to become global citizens.

Egypt: The Revolution Continues

Right after the Arab Spring broke up, the Leatherby Libraries Arts Exhibits and Events committee decided to respond to the world events and put together an exhibit of a dramatic photo display showcasing the work of a photojournalist killed while covering the civil war in Syria.

"Egypt: The Revolution Continues" (Egypt: the revolution continues, 2014) (see Figure 6.3) features the work of Ali Mustafa, a Toronto photojournalist killed in March while covering a government bombing in Aleppo, according to the Associated Press. A free reception and talk about the Arab Spring by Chapman Faculty Dr. Ahmed Younis was delivered.

"Collaboration" was the theme of this event. The library partnered with academic units from across the Chapman community, Egypt Cancer Network, the Center for Global Education, and the departments of English, History, and Political Science.

Figure 6.2 Dr. Bhagat Singh Thind Archives Exhibition

Figure 6.3 An image of the Arab Spring in Tahrir Square captured by the late Ali
Mustafa is among the featured photographs in the Leatherby Libraries
exhibition Egypt: The Revolution Continues.

Empowering Muslim Women Exhibit and Program

The goal of the program was to exhibit a carefully curated display of 20 trusted and well-researched academic books by world-acclaimed authors, as well as inviting the students to engage in private conversations with the speaker and some of the Muslim women in attendance. During the program, Lobna Youssef Mulla, one of the leading Muslim women in Southern California and a Chapman University student at the time, spoke about the realities of Muslim women and dispelled some of the common misunderstandings people have about their lives (Bonker, D. 2013). Even though Muslim women were empowered more than 1,400 years ago with rights to education, inheritance, and the freedom of marriage and divorce, so many people still have misconceptions about them and the rights they have in Islam to this day. After the presentation, attendees also browsed a display titled, "Empowering Muslim Women." (see Figure 6.4) showcasing examples of powerful Muslim women throughout history from the early times of Islam to the contemporary world. Free headscarves and beads were available, and the students watched a live demo on how to wrap a headscarf, took pictures, and enjoyed some Middle Eastern food. The program was open to all the Chapman University Staff, Faculty, and community in a step toward answering their questions and engaging with the speaker. Following the panel, some of the students reached out to the speaker and other attendees to continue the conversation. Some of the senior students conducted interviews for their senior theses with some of the Muslim women employees and students on campus. They asked them about their experiences and life. The program and the exhibit were later replicated at some other local Junior colleges and Universities in collaboration with the Leatherby Libraries.

Campus Pride Month at the Leatherby Libraries

April is Campus Pride Month, and here at the Leatherby we show our pride and work closely with the Civic Engagement office to engage students and promote understanding (Karas, R., n.d.a).

Additionally, National Pride Month takes place in June, but since most colleges and universities are done for the school year by June, April was selected specifically for Campus Pride Month. The goal of Campus Pride Month is to show support for the Lesbian, Gay, Bisexual, Transgender, and Queer (LGBTQ) community, as well as provide education and understanding about LGBTQ issues in an effort to promote acceptance. Our support is usually apparent on the inside and the outside of the library on the outside we have hung a large rainbow flag (see Figure 6.5).

Inside the lobby of the library, we have a yearly book display for Campus Pride Month (see Figure 6.6). Librarians or Library staff and students select a wide array of materials dealing with LGBTQ issues and decorated with flags for the different communities. The case usually includes a rainbow

Figure 6.4 Empowering Muslim Women, a program and book display that was sponsored by the Leatherby Libraries at Chapman University to help expose common misconceptions relating to women in Islam through sharing correct information.

pride flag, as well as several other less well-known flags. These new flags represent other identities within the LGBTQ community: transgender, bisexual, polysexual, and asexual. There are usually books, DVDs, and even musical scores! All these items are usually available for check out through the Circulation desk.

Figure 6.5 Our support for Campus Pride month is apparent on the outside of the library too! On the outside, we have hung a large rainbow flag in collaboration with the Civic Engagement office, The LGBTQIA+ Staff & Faculty Forum.

Figure 6.6 Inside the library, we have a book display for Campus Pride Month. Librarian David Carson selected a wide array of materials dealing with LGBTQ issues. There were books, DVDs, and even musical scores. These items are usually available for check out at the circulation desk.

Celebrating Ethnic Studies and Latinx Art Exhibit

The Leatherby Libraries is a proud sponsor of the yearly Education and Ethnic Studies Summit. A one-day summit that features nationally recognized experts in the Ethnic Studies field as well as community activists and leaders with the theme, "Nurturing Community: Critical Consciousness, Spirituality, and Solidarity." In collaboration with the Donna Ford Attallah College of Educational Studies and the Office of Diversity & Inclusion (Atalla College, n.d) the library hosts a yearly youth art exhibition, Mi Cultura es mi Poder (My Culture is my Power) featuring works by Hispanic students from local Middle and High Schools (Wogahn, M. 2018). This exhibition is part of Chapman University's annual Education and Ethnic Studies Summit. The Summit features nationally recognized experts in the Ethnic Studies field as well as community activists and leaders with the theme, "Nurturing Community: Critical Consciousness, Spirituality, and Solidarity." During the reception, visitors enjoy refreshments as they explore colorful paintings that celebrate cultural identity and community. Students also get the opportunity to speak about the project and its importance. Recently the library also decided to hang a flag in support of the Ethnic Studies program at Chapman University (see Figure 6.7).

Figure 6.7 The library demonstrates its commitment to the Ethnic Studies Minor by displaying an Ethnic Studies flag.

A Country Called Syria

The "A Country Called Syria" exhibit was hosted after the war broke out in Syria in 2015 (see Figure 6.8). It was a reminder of lives, culture, and a future at risk in a devastated nation. This exhibition showcased artifacts from Syrian culture and was co-curated by Maria Khani, a Syrian woman living in Orange County, and her daughter Dania Alkhouli, also an Orange County resident. The exhibit immersed guests into the culture of a country far away. The exhibit consisted of artifacts such as art, clothing, instruments, and a picture of Khani's parents and it demonstrated the human side of the country (Bonker, D. 2015). Without getting into the political crisis, the exhibit tried to shed light on the history, the culture, and the treasures of the country many don't know is the cradle of civilization. The library along with the owners of the artifacts displayed the collection as something that could show visitors a different perspective of Syria.

The exhibit was focused on bringing an exhibit to campus that will offer students global understanding, which is the mission of Chapman University. While "A Country Called Syria" has traveled to various museums around Southern California, this was the first time it was being shown in an academic setting. The exhibit opening brought over 75 people who were served a traditional Middle Eastern food from a local sponsor, Aleppo's Kitchen, a Mediterranean/Middle East-style restaurant and attendees were able to get their name written in Arabic calligraphy. The audience also heard remarks from the curators as well as from a local woman Lynn Matthews, who had another concurrent exhibit in the library featuring art exchanged between

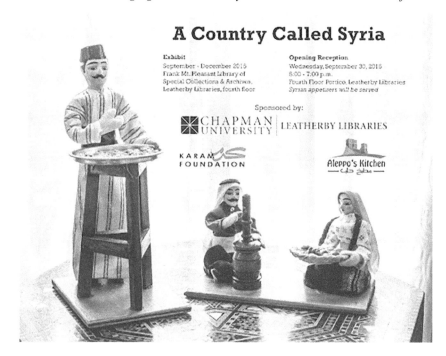

Figure 6.8 The reception included a talk by curators Maria and Dania Al Khouli and Syrian American artist Kinda Hibrawi.

children in the United States and refugee camps in the Middle East. As a result of this collaboration, "A Country Called Syria" was featured in local and regional newspapers and radio stations and later traveled to other academic institutions such as the University of California, Berkley, and California State University, Fullerton.

Portrait of a People: A Jewish Heritage Exhibit

To engage in interfaith and interreligious discussion, the library hosted a Jewish exhibition sponsored by donor Constance Harris. The exhibition featured objects on loan that were originally donated to the University of Michigan Library by Ms. Harris and the late Theodore Harris of Beverly Hills, who in late 2003 and early 2004 gave the university their extraordinary collection of more than 2,000 Jewish heritage items (Bonker. D, 2012). The collection reflects contemporary and past Jewish life in an unusual assemblage of artwork, books, printed ephemera such as pamphlets (see Figure 6.9) and postcards, and objects of everyday and religious significance, including toys, dolls, serving dishes, menorahs, and mezuzahs. The exhibit also included personal items from the Harris family, along with a New Year pop-up card contributed by Chapman's Frank Mt. Pleasant

About the Speakers

Julye Bidmead

Julye Bidmead (Ph.D., Vanderbilt University) is an Assistant Professor of Religious Studies. She is the author of *The Akitu Festival: Religious Continuity and Royal Legitimation in Mesopotamia* (Gorgias Press, 2002). Dr. Bidmead has been on the staff of numerous archaeological excavations in Israel, including the Megiddo Expedition. She teaches courses in Hebrew Bible, biblical archaeology, and gender studies at Chapman University.

About Constance Harris

Constance (Connie) Harris was born into the family of Nell and Henry Fedcr in New York City, and attended Hunter College, majoring in English Literature. Connie became active in the Jewish Federation Council of Los Angeles, serving on a variety of committees and as President of the Women's Conference. She started a group known as the Women's Interfaith Committee with the purpose of fostering personal relationships so that participants put a face on religious outside their own and came to understand the best parts of each other's religious experiences. Connie Harris is generously sharing the Jewish art, books, and objects which have so interested her. Her intent is to sustain the Jewish heritage from generation to generation.

The Jewish Heritage Exhibit will be on display from March 1 to May 21, 2012 Leatherby Libraries, First Floor

The Michigan University Library and the Frankel Center for Judaic Studies are the joint beneficiaries of a generous gift from Constance and (the late) Theodore Harris of Beverly Hills, California, who in late 2003 and early 2004 gave an extraordinary collection of some 2000 items to the University of Michigan.

Chapman University, Leatherby Libraries
One University Drive, Orange, California 92866
(714) 532-7756   www.chapman.edu/library

CHAPMAN UNIVERSITY
LEATHERBY LIBRARIES

Cordially invites you and your guests to

PORTRAIT OF A PEOPLE:
A Jewish Heritage Exhibit

Reception and Program
March 14, 2012
6:30 to 8:30 p.m.

Chapman University
Doy and Dee Henley Reading Room
Leatherby Libraries, Second Floor

Please RSVP by March 9th
to Essraa Nawar at 714-532-7748
or nawar@chapman.edu

Vegetarian refreshments will be served

About the Speakers

Rabbi Elie Kaplan Spitz

Rabbi Elie Spitz has served Congregation Bnai Israel of Tustin for close to a quarter of a century. He is the author of two books—*Does the Soul Survive? A Jewish Journey to Belief in Afterlife, Past Lives*, and *Living with Purpose and Healing from Despair: Finding Wholeness in a Broken World*. He has served on the Conservative Movement's Committee of Jewish Law and Standard for fifteen years and is guest speaker at Chapman University on the Course on "The Writings of Elie Wiesel."

About the Exhibit

This exhibit is organized around three major themes to demonstrate the wide variety of topics that can be illuminated by studying materials in the Jewish Heritage Collection.

Themes of the Exhibit

Ritual objects in the home

Love and marriage

Children's life

About the Collection

The Jewish Heritage Collection Dedicated to Mark and Dave Harris was formed to reflect Jewish life, and it does so in an unusual assemblage of artwork, books, printed ephemera such as pamphlets and postcards, and objects of everyday and religious significance ranging from dolls and serving dishes to menorahs and mezuzahs.

The exhibit "Portrait of a People " was drawn from items donated by Constance Harris to the University of Michigan University Library for use by students, faculty and other scholars. Also, parts of the exhibit include personal items from the Harris family along with a New Year pop-up card contributed by the Frank Mt. Pleasant Library of Special Collections and Archives at Chapman University.

Figure 6.9 Portrait of a People: A Jewish Heritage Exhibit" – opened on March 14, 2012, with a program and reception in the Doy and Dee Henley Reading Room of the Leatherby Libraries.

Library of Special Collections and Archives. The exhibit was organized around three major themes: Ritual Objects in the Home, Love and Marriage, and Children's Life. Speakers at the opening reception included the donor, Constance Harris, along with Rabbi Elie Kaplan Spitz of Congregation B'nai Israel of Tustin and Julye Bidmead, Ph.D., assistant professor of religious studies.

Book Displays

The Leatherby Libraries is committed to showcase its diverse collections and resources through year-round book displays that respond to local or international events, celebrate a campus event, or collaborate with a campus department or group. These displays included but were not limited to:

- Banned book display.
- National poetry month displays.
- Death of local poets/writers.
- Nelson Mandela's death through a library display.
- Visits by Nobel Laureates such as Elie Wiesel.
- Death of Omar Sharif.
- Celebrating ten years of the Arabic Studies Program at Chapman University.
- Interfaith celebration display.
- Refugees artists work.
- Release of Star Wars movies.

Ensuring Attendance and Outreach: Leatherby Libraries Marketing Plan

The Leatherby Libraries follows a certain process in the promotion of its diverse activities, exhibits, and events; to complement the Library's Strategic Plan; and to assist the libraries and the university's faculty, staff, students, and the larger community in understanding the tactics, strategy, and procedures related to the marketing of its events, activities, resources, and awards. The Leatherby Libraries play an integral role in the university's teaching, learning, and research. The library's vision and mission statements enforce the library's increasing leadership role in the life and culture of the campus and community.

Marketing Events and Exhibits in Academic Libraries

Just like corporations and start-ups, libraries of all kinds need to invest time, energy, and resources on their marketing strategies. By applying some of these techniques, libraries will not just be able to better understand their users' needs but also secure more funding, communicate effectively to their

internal and external constituents, and more importantly ensure attendance for their educational events and exhibits. The Leatherby Libraries has
a robust Marketing Strategy that was developed in 2011. This strategy continues to be refined and updated yearly to reflect the newest and the latest
trends and lessons learned from previous years.

Objectives of the Marketing Plan

- Continually promote the mission and goals of the Leatherby Libraries
  to internal and external entities in order to enhance the image of the
  Leatherby Libraries and increase the visibility of the library and its
  value in the Chapman University community.
- Developing and implementing marketing, branding, and communications practices to support the Leatherby Libraries strategic plan in
  attracting faculty, staff, students, and other entities on and off campus,
  as required.
- Provide support for the planning, coordination, and execution of projects,
  events, promotions, and other marketing-related activities. Including, but
  not limited to exhibitions, lectures, receptions, book signing/talks, semi-
  nars, retreats, book sales, donor-related activities, and festivals.
- Manage all social media marketing efforts, including writing and managing content, following Chapman University social media policies
  and procedures, and attracting students. This includes the Leatherby
  Libraries Facebook Page, Instagram feed and bi-monthly e-newsletters
  (launched Fall 2019), blog posts, and weekly internal newsletters.
- Develop and manage all the recurring publications such as the Leatherby
  Libraries Annual Report as well as various newsletters, brochures,
  posters, signage, and trifolds.
- Development and design of marketing materials throughout the academic year for advertisements, newsletters, direct mail, and public relations materials.
- Increase the awareness of the community of the benefit of the library
  activities and services.
- Increase the level of participation of Chapman University alums and
  community members in the life of the university and stimulate the
  donation and gifting process.
- Increase the level of satisfaction among our students, faculty, staff, and
  community members.
- Develop and maintain effective working relationships with internal and
  external media entities, ensuring maximum visibility of the Leatherby
  Libraries on campus as well as in local media outlets (see "Marketing
  and Communication Outlets" on pages 83–84).
- Increase the level of participation of Chapman University alums and
  community members in the life of the university and stimulate the
  donation and gifting process.

- Increase awareness of the library's digital collections by collaborating with the Scholarly Communications librarian, Chapman University Digital Commons, the Office of Undergraduate Research, Strategic Marketing and Communications, and outside organizations to highlight and promote digital collections.

Strategies

To promote the Leatherby Libraries services, resources, and activities, the library will undertake the following strategies:

- Increase the visibility of library resources through the library website, brochures, social networking tools, and other appropriate marketing and communication channels.
- Identify services and collections to highlight through a program, event, display, and/or exhibition.
- Sponsor special events in coordination with other colleges and departments.
- Raise awareness of the library's digital resources through flyers, blog posts, press releases, events, and links on social media that focus on the digital resources and the library's Digital Commons database.
- Sponsor and support external speakers, exhibitions, and programs that highlight the Leatherby Libraries' diverse collection and activities.
- Establish new community partnerships to support speakers and activities that strengthen relationships between the university and local businesses and non-profit organizations (e.g., bookstores, museums and public libraries, embassies, cultural institutes, etc.).
- Highlight the research, scholarly accomplishments, and professional contributions of Leatherby Libraries librarians and staff through the Chapman University website, library website, and Facebook page.
- Sponsor tours and activities for on-campus and off-campus groups to raise awareness of the library.
- Develop online content (blog posts, virtual exhibits, digital photo albums, web flyers, and graphics) to provide patrons with helpful information and to attract their interest in the library. Share this content via social media, the library website, university-wide online marketing channels, and other methods as needed.
- Continually assess our marketing techniques for efficacy in achieving our goals and make changes to strategy and tactics in response to the results of our assessments.

Marketing and Communication Outlets

- Press releases and articles
- Informational flyers

- Posters
- Advertisements
- Announcements
- Newsletters
- Brochures
- Library guides
- Social networking tools (Facebook, Instagram)
- "Leatherby Libraries Year in Review" (Annual Report) – discontinued in 2015
- Presentations
- Website highlights
- "Digital Signage" Marketing Screens
- The Panther Newspaper
- Chapman University Newsroom
- Chapman University Magazine
- Chapman University Calendar (events.chapman.edu)
- Chapman University section of the Orange County Register
- Other opportunities that occur through Chapman University Strategic Marketing and Communications (SMC) such as web interviews, TV interviews, external blogs, etc.
- Partnerships with on-campus/off-campus entities.
- Library packets
- Bookmarks
- Exhibition booklets
- Stories and event notifications posted using Chapman's blogging tools
- Email newsletters to donors and friends of the library on a bi-monthly basis via "campaign monitor" e-newsletter system
- Submitting our events to academic journals such as ACRL
- Weekly Internal Newsletter: This Week in the Library

Conclusion and Commitment to Reimagining Diversity, Equity, and Inclusion

Diversity is the buzzword of the century, and a great amount of important work has been done on DEI in recent years, but we have hit an upper limit and it is time to continue to reimagine and redefine diversity as new generations and new demographics of students attend college and more factors come into play. We cannot rely on conventional methods and strategies anymore. Thus, the Leatherby Libraries' commitment to bringing authentic and diverse displays, exhibits, and events to life is a genuine step toward this commitment. Exhibits, programming, and events hosted by the Leatherby Libraries often introduce patrons to diverse experiences, values, and worldviews that go beyond their classroom experience. Through these exhibits and events, the library helps to deepen the institutional commitment to inquiry and inclusiveness, among other values.

References

Attallah College of Education Studies. (n.d.). *Education & Ethnic Studies Summit.* Chapman University. https://www.chapman.edu/education/events/ethnic-studies.aspx

Bonker, D. (2012, March 19). Home life, marriage, children focus of Jewish Heritage exhibit at Leatherby Libraries. *Chapman University Newsroom.* https://news.chapman.edu/2012/03/19/home-life-marriage-children-focus-of-jewish-heritage-exhibit-at-leatherby-libraries/

Bonker, D. (2013, March 1). The real lives of Muslim women to be topic of Leatherby Libraries guest speaker. *Chapman University Newsroom.* https://news.chapman.edu/2013/03/01/the-real-lives-of-muslim-women-to-be-topic-of-leatherby-libraries-event/

Bonker, D. (2015, September 22). "A Country Called Syria": An exhibit at Leatherby Libraries is a reminder of lives, culture and a future at stake in devastated nation. *Chapman University Newsroom.* https://news.chapman.edu/2015/09/22/a-country-called-syria/

Egypt: The Revolution Continues. (2014, September 24). *Chapman University Digital Commons.* https://digitalcommons.chapman.edu/egypt_the_revolution_continues/

Karas, R. (2021, February 23). Leatherby Libraries Wins Award for Diversity Initiative. *Leatherby Libraries Blog.* https://blogs.chapman.edu/library/2021/02/23/leatherby-libraries-wins-award-for-diversity-initiative/

Karas, R. (n.d.a). *Celebrating LGBTQIA+ Pride Month at the Leatherby Libraries.* https://scalar.chapman.edu/scalar/celebrating-lgbtq-pride-month-at-the-leatherby-libraries/index

Karas, R. (n.d.b) Sikhs and Sikhism in America Group Study Room. *Telling Stories: One Room at a Time.* https://scalar.chapman.edu/scalar/leatherby-libraries-story-rooms/sikhs-and-sikhism-in-america-group-study-room

Ross, K., & Nawar, E. (2021, June). *Reimagining diversity at the Leatherby Libraries: A strategy for success* [presentation]. ALA Annual Conference and Exhibition Virtual. https://digitalcommons.chapman.edu/library_presentations/31/

Turban Display. (2014, May 1). *Chapman University Digital Commons.* https://digitalcommons.chapman.edu/turban_display/

Wogahn, M. (2018, April 30). Mi Cultura es mi Poder (My Culture is my Power). *Leatherby Libraries Blog.* https://blogs.chapman.edu/library/2018/04/30/mi-cultura-es-mi-poder/

7 Environmental Equity for Students in the Library and LEED Buildings

Peggy Cabrera and Elizabeth A. Carroll

SJSU Librarian's Experience

As a life-long library user and academic librarian, I know libraries contribute to community equity through access to information across all disciplines and interests. My discovery of other ways libraries increase equity began when I became the liaison to the Environmental Studies department and joined the University's Sustainability Board. Not having formal training in environmental studies or sustainability, but having grown up in a low-income household like many San José State University (SJSU) students, I wanted to contribute to student understanding of sustainability and climate change. Embedding sustainability into campus curriculum was a frequent topic of the faculty on the SJSU Sustainability Board like on many college campuses (AASHE Campus Sustainability Hub, 2021; Reynolds, 2010). As a librarian who teaches mostly "one shot" information literacy classes, I could encourage students to reuse library books and research from home to save money and time. Believing that the library could play a more prominent role in sustainability on campus, I set out to find a way.

After seeing a presentation on the King Library's Leadership in Energy & Environmental Design (LEED) certification, I began exploring how students could learn about sustainable buildings. I learned about LEED, its certification process, and the library's sustainable features. When the "Campus as a Living Lab" (CALL) grant was discussed at the Sustainability Board, I recognized an opportunity (California State University, 2014). I envisioned designing a module for faculty to teach students about how the King Library's sustainable features provide environmental equity for its users. Students could apply this information to the buildings in their home and work lives. Working with the SJSU Environmental Studies department chair, three sites were selected as living labs. As the grant proposal awarded extra points to campuses that partnered with local community colleges, faculty from environmental studies and horticultural programs at the local community colleges were invited to join, resulting in nine living lab modules, three per campus, which became available for faculty from all three campuses to adopt.

DOI: 10.4324/9781003167174-8

In 2014, I created the King Library LEED Certification module using the Springshare software to provide long-term access for the SJSU and general community (Cabrera, 2014). Except for the subscription databases, anyone can access the LEED module's content.

Other design decisions included short text blocks, links to library history, SJSU library and sustainability videos, and quick polls on personal choices (transportation, water use, energy use, materials use) for student reflection. Students were encouraged to tag photos of the library's features online. As students tour the building, they score their assigned credit as certified, silver, gold, or platinum using a blank rubric with the points listed for each level. Students are asked to make a holistic evaluation based on what they see, feel, hear, and touch, and not on the LEED points system. The points are included to help students understand the differences between the credit ratings. A group studying water efficiency identifies where water is used inside and outside the building, who uses it, how it is used, evidence of recycled or grey water, and the design of the water use feature. The goal is to focus students' critical thinking on the effectiveness of the building's design and sustainable features. A link to the library's LEED scores is available for students to see the points each credit earned (SJSU, Facilities Development & Operations, 2010). Through this hands-on activity, students transition from passive building users to informed users knowing its design, operations, and maintenance.

To introduce faculty from the three campuses to the curriculum, an orientation session was held to share the modules and to answer participation and grant stipend questions. From the start, Carroll indicated her interest in the King Library as a LEED building module. Discussion of the module's content between us occurred through email as Carroll prepared to include it in her curriculum. I was surprised when Carroll asked me to introduce the module to students, as I had thought my involvement would end when faculty embedded the module into their courses. Her invitation has increased my skills teaching LEED, and sustainability, thus deepening my content knowledge. The students share how they think about sustainability, and they continually surprise us with the creative and interdisciplinary approaches to their presentations. My teaching skills and awareness of students' needs have grown from the partnership with Carroll and her classes.

SJSU Art History Faculty's Experience

As academics, we have an awareness that curriculum choices and content delivery can reveal much about the instructor and department. However, even more critical is the student-centered experience that gives rise to an engaged learning environment. With these thoughts in mind, when I began teaching ARTH 72 "Design in Society," I questioned: how would I effectively reach a large lecture class of students from differing cultural experiences all mixed into one?[1] The heterogeneity of ARTH 72 students motivated me to explore changes within the GE design history curriculum.[2] The aim was twofold: one, to foster student interactivity and engagement, and two, equity in performance and merit. Part of this curriculum "awareness" was to acknowledge that Art and Design History curricula can project hierarchical perspectives that distort racial and cultural identities. Because design histories are object-, space- and project-based, there are always "biases of which we are not aware...an issue that haunts all cultural studies" (Prown, 2000, 25). I wanted to create a design curriculum that students could learn through "hands-on" interaction. The CSU CALL Faculty Workshop offered a solution to the project-based assignment I had envisioned. The King Library LEED Certification Module could be adapted to introduce sustainable design that builds toward a concluding assignment on LEED certification at the library. While the teaching module adoption demanded effort, the results would be vital to engaging students in the process of self-discovery, the hands-on element, and learning about sustainably built construction on campus. I embedded the teaching module into my syllabus, and by the end of the process, the King Library Sustainable Design Group assignment was born. Onsite visits, a fundamental requirement, would compel students to investigate King Library LEED features through visual observations of design.

Collaborative Choreography: Faculty Reflections

Promoting student collaboration is hard to do successfully – which is what we learned when we participated in the SJSU eCampus active learning workshop in 2017. Group learning doesn't happen on its own. If we want authentic collaboration, we must intentionally and consistently build it into our learning activities. One of the lessons learned is that students don't generally collaborate on simple tasks. However, when there is complexity, it becomes stimulating and requires "positive interdependence" (Johnson et al., 1998, pp. 8–10). LEED principles challenge students, and the on-campus activity encourages reliance on one another. The exercise would have certain requirements, which could be described as "decision-making, trust-building, communication, and conflict-management skills" (Johnson et al., 1998, p. 7). The assignment would be designed with "mutual goals, shared resources, joint rewards and assigned roles" (p. 7) to make the group learning successful. In the aim of coalescing students, it would be necessary to continuously mediate the cooperative structure with shorter-term goals and deadlines to "structure interdependence" (p. 14).

Face-to-face and online synchronous classes will often favor an environment whereby students are seated next to each other yet focus on their own individual devices, or the same is true with breakout rooms. Their preference might be to work toward their own individual goals instead of a collaborative task, unless there is enough complexity. Students were divided into groups of five or more people and then required to scrutinize, observe, document, research, write and present on six LEED categories: Sustainable Sites, Location and Transportation, Water Efficiency, Energy and Atmosphere, Materials and Resources, and Indoor Environmental Quality. With explanation of the task, group roles would be self-selected and then assigned to ensure accountability and positive cooperation. This culminating assignment requires constant modeling, monitoring, and intervention with groups. A few semesters into this assignment, we created opportunities for peer review and self-evaluation so students could recognize success or where improvement was needed. Essentially, this assignment like other aspects of instruction would require constant revision for the technical aspects of LEED that evolve and to keep the material fresh.

As our faculty collaboration evolved, we aligned our goals in instructional planning, which were: firstly, to increase basic knowledge of sustainability as defined by the 1987 Brundtland Commission, "... meeting the needs of the present without compromising the ability of future generations ...," (World Commission on Environment and Development, 1987) and secondly, to connect students to sustainable design approaches, and thirdly, to gain experience in a collaborative group environment. By Fall 2014, the King Library LEED Certification module was fully integrated into ARTH 72 and ready for instruction. The module initiates with the introduction of "ecologically intentional design" (Stegall, 2006) during week 7 of the 16-week semester. By week 8, we introduce the global picture of sustainability to then make it local by defining LEED and how to learn from the SJSU campus. In effect, students are taught sustainable design through lecture and "active learning" content, readings, discussion, and a culminating collaborative project.

Collaborative Choreography: Librarian's Reflections

Every semester as a guest lecturer in the ARTH 72 sections, I ask students about their definitions of sustainability to understand what students know. Many students have heard of sustainability through news, social media, and the youth environmental movement in the United States and abroad. When asked, they list the environment, saving resources, money, or efficiency as important to sustainability, yet equity is rarely identified. To help students visualize sustainability's three main concepts – equity, environment, and economics – I ask students to guess what the images embedded in the module represent. Once they identify the group image as a community, the concept becomes clearer–equity includes everyone.

The layout of the LibGuide's tabs and content function as the in-class lesson plan. After sustainability, the class discusses building usage with data from the Bureau of Labor documenting the time people spend at work, home, and leisure (Bureau of Labor Statistics, 2019) and includes a chart focusing on students' use of time, "Time use on an average weekday for full-time university and college students," (Bureau of Labor Statistics, n.d.).

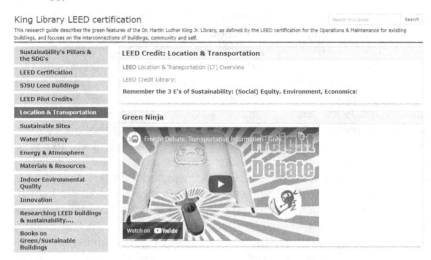

Figure 7.1 King Library LEED Module Content, LEED Certification LibGuide, "Location and Transportation," Information

Besides the number of hours spent in buildings, students count how many buildings they occupy daily (home, campus, work, social). Students' awareness of the importance of buildings grows by reflecting on the buildings in their daily routines.

The LibGuide includes many resources for students. A brief video introduces LEED and its history. Each LEED credit has a tab linking to the LEED credit library and supporting materials. "Green Ninja" videos offer students a fun (see Figure 7.1), visual mode to learn through peer teaching as SJSU's Animation students and faculty created many of them (Green Ninja, 2010). Other tabs feature newer campus LEED-certified buildings, research information including databases, books on green buildings, and LEED test books for students wanting to earn LEED accreditation. When new versions of LEED are released, the LibGuide is updated. LEED v.2 was the standard when the LibGuide was created. The LEED version used for each building is included for students' comparison. Students learn how to use LEED's credit library to find the required versions (U.S. Green Building Council, 2021).

Lessons Learned: What Students Taught Us

Surveys

We began to survey students before the module, and after their group presentations with IRB approval to learn if our learning objectives for students had been met. Our survey goals were to learn if students could fully define sustainability and evaluate changes in their consumer behaviors after studying the module. We wanted to learn if students could recall the LEED credit

LEED certification is based on seven major categories. What categories would you create to rate a building on its sustainability?	
Transportation & Location	45 (26)
Sustainable Sites	28 (12)
Water Efficiency	54 (36)
Energy & Atmosphere	63 (11)
Materials & Resources	51 (15)
Indoor Environmental Quality	47 (4)
Innovation	15 (3)
Miscellaneous	15

Figure 7.2 Student Recall of LEED Credits

Note: (#) represents the number of students who recalled the exact names of the LEED credits. The larger number represents the combined students with exact and near recall of LEED credit names.

names to demonstrate their learning about LEED (Figure 7.2). We required students to apply the sustainable design theories to their analysis of the library and LEED credit in their group work. When asked to define the three E's of Sustainability, more students identified economics and environment yet had difficulty recalling social equity. However, their presentations would reveal library users other than SJSU students, such as children, families, and the homeless. Students were asked two questions regarding design; one: how could ecologically intentional design be used at King Library? We received a narrow range of answers specifically connected to sustainable practices at King Library. At the same time, students supplied a much broader range of general answers such as "it makes students feel at home," or "it could remind the user of waste or unsustainable behavior," and "it could preserve the building while tending to the community, and it could create design that "doesn't feel stuffy." And the second design question: "how can designed features like what you experience in indoor environmental quality, water efficiency, materials, energy & atmosphere, and/or signage help communicate the message to users about sustainability?" The vast majority of students provided a variety of answers about the communication of sustainable design in that it was easier to use, can be done with art, and can teach others to save resources through the use of graphic designs in posters, signs, and pictures.

Student Presentations

In presentations, students discuss the LEED credits and building features that affect their health, such as the Energy and Atmosphere of the library, and the benefits of the library's windows and the glass atrium designed for daytime lighting for students to study. They mention the motion-controlled stacks lighting as one way the library conserves energy yet provides light for students searching for books. Depending on the floors students use in the library, students can select a study environment that works best for their needs between cooler temperatures to remain alert and warmer floors when they are feeling cold. Students recognize the library's "Indoor Environmental Quality" because the air conditioning filtration system limits outside smells and interior dust. Discussions of the Water Efficiency credit frequently describe California's droughts and limited rainfall. Some students describe exterior water use including French drainage for landscaping and stormwater management. The Materials & Resources credit groups highlight the use of non-toxic cleaning solutions, floor mats to catch incoming dirt and dust, and the library's bins for recycling paper and plastic. Students like the library's goal to clean and reupholster furniture. Reuse of books and media for check-out or for sale in the library's bookstore often appears in their slides. Students studying the Sustainable Site credit mention the local cafes and businesses that serve campus. The library's proximity to public transportation (buses, light rail, parking) makes it accessible for everyone, and its elevators, escalators, stairs, and wide walkways increase access for diverse users.

One credit, Water Efficiency, stands out because of students' responses. Since Fall 2014, student submissions have documented King Library in both photography and video to illustrate their interpretations of eco-efficient design. Their exploration of water efficiency posits that Mel Chin's, "Reflecting Pools" sinks are the ideal visual manifestation to advocate water conservation in the library restrooms (Figure 7.3). Reflecting on what

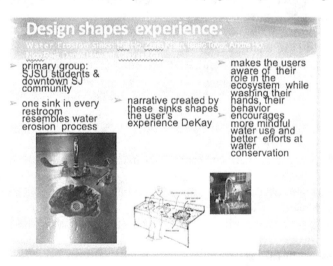

Figure 7.3 Water Efficiency Presentation Slide (Gu et al., 2017) – Application of DeKay's theory

Note: Application of DeKay's theory.

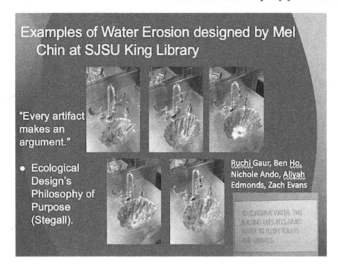

Figure 7.4 Water Efficiency Presentation Slide – Application of Stegall's theory

Note: Application of Stegall's theory.

students learned from integrated readings (DeKay, 2012; McDonough, 2002; Stegall, 2006; Thomashow, 2014), the design itself serves an argument for how people should behave. The sink design demonstrates a sense of accountability and connection to nature. In the case of "Reflecting Pools," the hollowed-out erosion patterns that form the sink basins are evidence of "people in a sustainable society ... a spiritual connection and sense of stewardship"(Stegall, 2006, p. 60). As the library user travels from floors 8 to 3, the restroom sink basins increase in breadth to illustrate erosion's impact. According to students' on-site observations, users entered and exited restrooms, yet it was apparent that the eroded sink design was not attention-grabbing, much less inspiring people to use less water. Disappointingly, the design was not impacting the end user regarding eco-efficient use of water, "... it ... feels as though a point has been missed. They bring awareness, however as a student and user, I wish there was a sign or placard, explaining these awesome sinks" (Gaur et al., 2016). As seen in Figure 7.4, King Library has signage acknowledging its use of reclaimed water, which links to the ideas of Mitchell Thomashow, that the campus should "serve as a studio for practicing sustainable initiatives" (Thomashow, 2014, pp. 9–10, 16). This one example demonstrates how San José State students have interpreted LEED design and practice at King Library.[3]

(Re)Activating a Green Curriculum

Our next phase of guiding students to the learning objectives took shape when we joined an active learning strategies faculty cohort. One immediate change was to broaden the students' perspective from focusing solely on the King Library to including new LEED buildings such as the Student Union (a partial remodel with new wings) and the Student Wellness Center. One reason to redesign the assignment was to better meet students' needs since not all students use the library to study. In fact, a majority use the Student Union. The Student Wellness Center offers multiple health services for all SJSU students. We asked students to make onsite visits to the library and newer LEED buildings to discover their interior design features. In this way, students could improve their critical thinking skills by comparing and contrasting the library to the newer campus LEED buildings. We wanted students to apply sustainable design theory to other buildings to reinforce their awareness of how building designs can change over time in response to newer technologies and design features.

Other curriculum changes included broadening group roles and presentation responses. In 2017, we created formal roles for the students such as a content manager to manage the overall presentation content and an images manager. The image manager was responsible for sourcing photos used in their presentations. Depending on the group's size, the roles could be shared. The goal in formalizing these roles was to give all students duties in the final group presentation and paper. Creating opportunities for groups to get responses from multiple perspectives was the other major change. The next step was to build mandatory peer review feedback on group presentations for all students. This change required students to pay attention to their peers' presentations. Using SJSU's Learning Management System (LMS), Canvas, we designed a survey tool where students respond to the group collectively and individually and ask questions with the aim of improvement. Presentation responses have a deadline within one half hour of the class conclusion so that presentations are fresh in the minds of reviewers. We envisioned peer-review and self-assessment requirements that would create an opportunity for students to think critically about their LEED credit in addition to others. While students learn indirectly from each other's presentations, our retrospective impression is that the exercise generates a community for students within their own teams. Collaborating as a group requires communication, leadership, reflection, and working through problems. Consequently, student feedback from Spring 2021 suggests that closer guidance of what is called "process group functioning" (Johnson et al., 1998, p. 17) is a valuable next step. The feedback indicates some students struggled with communication, dedication to the project, and consistency over the two-month period. Student–Instructor dialogue in the form of celebration (what went well) with a pause for improvement (what could grow) would be a future intermediate step before the project conclusion. The goal of equity and inclusion here is about the student experience and needs of the individual: student feedback brings an asset.

We offered blended feedback from both of us, which has enabled us to focus our individual expertise related to the assignment requirements. We addressed thesis development and application of design theory features relevant to the LEED credit. We drew attention to the groups' analysis of the LEED credit to the buildings and inclusion of social equity analysis.

A major benefit of giving students blended feedback before the deadline ensures that they meet important assignment requirements.

Transitioning Through the Pandemic

Revisions were made to the curriculum with the aim of increasing student access to building information in Fall 2020. These changes were a direct response to campus closure during the pandemic. Simply, students could not visit SJSU's campus LEED buildings; thus the LibGuide necessitated additional links to building information. Students were directed to search Google Images and other social media sites to find images and videos for their research. To manage this new crowd-sourced content we created new roles to organize the additional content: a research tracker, image coordinator and web site coordinator.

In Spring 2021, we adopted two of LEED's pilot credits into the curriculum and module, Social Equity in the Community, and Safety First: Re-enter your Workplace. We simplified the related analysis tools for students' use. We selected the Social Equity in the Community credit to focus students' attention on understanding who is impacted by a building's construction, operations & management. Students analyze groups impacted by a building: general community, regular building users, service staff, and building visitors. They select one group from each of these categories and identify their basic demographic data, their relationship to the building, and the social equity issues the group may experience. In this way students are asked to draw on existing knowledge of who might use the building or to do some basic research about the building and the community. Finally, students choose one group to focus a social equity lens on to consider how partnerships can be created to minimize the impact new buildings have on a community.

Building on their study of this community, the pilot credit, Safety First: Re-enter your workplace, continued students' analysis of how their chosen community group can return to using the selected building safely. In this way, students identified the needs of this group and considered how building management meets their safety needs. Like other campuses, SJSU students will return in phases to campus for the Spring 2022 semester, so this analysis is timely. Our goal is that students will notice the intentional design in operations and maintenance that enables the public to use a building: from the signage; increased air circulation, cleaning, and maintenance of the spaces; access to water; and policies related to personal protection equipment and building use as campus seeks to increase access for students, staff, faculty, and the community-at-large.

Future Directions

The aforementioned pilot credits are new to the ARTH 72 curriculum, and we look forward to learning how students interact with them as they study about SJSU's LEED buildings. We anticipate approaching this analysis

Figure 7.5 AR App Mock-Up "Secrets of King Library" – Rules

using a couple of tools. First, we will survey students for their responses to these pilot credits. We want to understand if the modified tools succeeded in student comprehension of social equity. Second, the student presentations will allow us to assess how students applied this information to their analysis as well as a final exam question that requires an application of social equity.

Challenges in teaching the sustainability module lead us to consider future modifications. It has been a difficult task to introduce students to the technical concepts of LEED and to teach visualization of eco-efficient features in a high-performance building. The face-to-face curriculum begins with a library self-tour and a required activity. To this end, the tour serves as a start, yet the concepts and visualization of the interior features require repetition and reinforcement. Carroll's participation in an SJSU professional development workshop led to the idea of developing an app-based interactive, augmented reality (AR) treasure hunt-style exercise. The goal of developing an app is to improve student comprehension of green building features. Many students already work from their phones in lieu of a laptop; thus the app-based activity could improve student engagement[4] (Figures 7.5 and 7.6). While we developed a test version released to students in 2018, further development of the King Library virtual LEED tour is forthcoming and will benefit online learning. Since Fall 2020, the class has been taught virtually, which necessitates more visual documentation, online resources, and ideally a tour simulation.

Conclusion: LEED buildings and Your Campus

Today CALL modules can be adapted by any campus to use with their students. Our case study is an easy module to implement if one's campus has

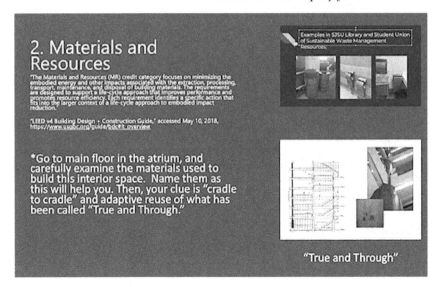

Figure 7.6 AR App Mock-Up "Secrets of King Library." – Materials and Resources

buildings certified by LEED or other green building standards. Using the library as a case study to compare to other LEED buildings allows students "to see" frequently used buildings through a sustainability and social equity lens. Beyond planning the curriculum, it is a matter of deciding what faculty want students to learn and which resources to use. Including information created by different campus offices can make it easier to organize some content. At SJSU, online content was part of the campus's community press releases, while the Office of Facilities Development & Operations and Office of Sustainability created websites about the Campus's LEED projects and the annual Sustainability reports. Creating a partnership with these offices on campus is important as they have access to information about a building's design, operations & maintenance that may not be available elsewhere. The Office of Sustainability can help promote collaboration across campus with other faculty, departments, and campus administration and may have information on related grants to support this work on campus.

Notes

1. ARTH 72 is a lower-division major requirement for all SJSU design students. *Design and Society* is likewise a university General Education course (Area C-1), reaching a diverse student spectrum. For SJSU demographics, see Office of Institutional Research, "Student Quick Facts" (Fall 2020) http://oir.sjsu.edu/Students/QuickFacts/.
2. San José State University General Education Requirements, (2020–2021), "... incorporates the development of skills, the acquisition of knowledge, and the integration of knowledge through the study of facts, issues, and ideas.

Regardless of major, all who earn undergraduate degrees would share common educational experiences as they become university scholars." https://catalog.sjsu.edu/preview_program.php?catoid=2&poid=450&returnto=96

3. A multitude of student presentations dating from Fall 2014 through Fall 2018 has been archived, which interpret the eco-efficient LEED categories at King Library. While the student responses are too vast to integrate into the present chapter, the commentary here is an effective representation.

4. In collaboration with Debbie Weissmann (SJSU School of Information), who offered to design the first part of "Secrets of King Library," students used the map-based AR app on campus in 2018. The game required students to complete a treasure hunt. As students completed steps in the treasure hunt, they uploaded photographs of the areas seen. Carroll asked them to photograph and film (in one case) the features relevant to the specific LEED category the student group was researching.

References

AASHE Campus Sustainability Hub. (2021). Association for Sustainability in Higher Education. https://hub.aashe.org/

Bureau of Labor Statistics. (2019). *American Time Use Survey, 2019 Results.* News release, Bureau of Labor Statistics, U.S. Department of Labor. Retrieved May 1, 2021 from https://www.bls.gov/news.release/pdf/atus.pdf

Bureau of Labor Statistics. (n.d.). *Time use on an average weekday for full-time university and college students.* Bureau of Labor Statistics, American Time Use Survey. https://www.bls.gov/tus/charts/chart6.pdf

Cabrera, P. (2014) *King library LEED certification.* Retrieved May 1, 2021 from https://Libguides.sjsu.edu/King_Library_Leed_certification

California State University. (2014). *"Campus as a Living Lab" Program.* (2014). CSU: The California State University. https://www2.calstate.edu/impact-of-the-csu/sustainability/Pages/Campus-as-a-Living-Lab.aspx

DeKay, M. (2012). "Five levels of sustainable design aesthetics: Perceiving and appreciating developmental complexity," *PLEA 2012: 28th Conference. Opportunities, Limits & Needs: Towards an Environmentally Responsible Architecture, Lima, Peru* 7–9 November 2012.

Gaur, R., Ho, B., Ando, N., Edmonds, A., & Evans, Z. (2016, May 10). *Water Efficiency. ARTH 72: Design in Society, Art & Art History Department.* CA: San José State University.

Gu, C., Ho, H., Khan, Z., Tovar, I., Ho, A., Reis, N., & Howard, D. (2017, May 15) *Water Efficiency, ARTH 72: Design in Society, Art & Art History Department.* : San José State University.

Green Ninja. (2010). *The Green Ninja Show [Video].* YouTube. https://www.youtube.com/user/GreenNinjaTV/featured

Johnson, R. T., Johnson, D. W., & Smith, K. A. (1998). *Active learning: Cooperation in the college classroom.* University of Minnesota.

McDonough, W., & Braungart, M. (2002). *Cradle to cradle: Remaking the way we make things.* Northpoint Press.

Prown, J. P. (2000). The truth of material culture: History or fiction? In J. P. Prown, & K. Haltman (Eds.), *American artifacts: Essays in material culture* (pp. 11–27). Michigan State University Press.

Reynolds, H. L. (2010). *Teaching environmental literacy: Across campus and across the curriculum.* Indiana University Press.

San Josè State University. (2020–2021). 2020–2021 Academic Catalog, "General Education Requirements." https://catalog.sjsu.edu

San José State University, Facilities Development & Operations (2010). Dr. Martin Luther King Jr. Library, Registered Building Checklist, Existing Buildings, https://www.sjsu.edu/fdo/docs/king_eb_checklist.pdf

San José State University, Office of Institutional Research. (Fall 2020). "Student Quick Facts." http://oir.sjsu.edu/Students/QuickFacts/

Stegall, N. (2006). Designing for sustainability: A philosophy for ecologically intentional design. *Design Issues, 22*(2), 56–63. Retrieved May 1, 2021, from http://www.jstor.org/stable/25224047

Thomashow, M. (2014). *The nine elements of a sustainable campus.* MIT Press.

U.S. Green Building Council. (2021). *LEED Credit Library.* Retrieved May 1, 2021 from https://www.usgbc.org/credits?Version=%22v4.1%22&Rating+System=%22New+Construction%22

World Commission on Environment and Development. (1987). Report of the World Commission in https://digitallibrary.un.org/record/139811?ln=en

8 Adhocking It: Overcoming the Overwhelm to Start Creating

Equitable and Inclusive Collections Now

Renae J. Watson, Khaleedah Thomas, and Kristine Nowak

Adhocking It: Overcoming the Overwhelm to Start Creating Equitable and Inclusive Collections Now

Along with their institutions, academic libraries are not immune to systemic issues of racism and bias. Historically, academic libraries have primarily collected Eurocentric scholarship written by white authors (Rapchak, 2019). Unfortunately, "[t]he overwhelming theme in conversation and in research regarding collection work is that librarians who undertake it just do not have time to reflect" or prioritize it in their long list of responsibilities (Berthoud & Finn, 2019, p. 165). Both time and potential overwhelm quickly became a stumbling block, too, for the Collections Diversity and Inclusion Group (CDIG), an ad-hoc task force of four library employees with support from our collections coordinator. The primary goal of CDIG is to collect and showcase works authored by, or that focus on, voices traditionally marginalized, or altogether excluded, from academic scholarship. Like many academic libraries at predominantly White institutions, Colorado State University (CSU) Libraries had developed collections to support the teaching and research needs of faculty and students, including those in Ethnic Studies and Women's Studies, but collecting had not been equitable; we realized our library must do better.

When getting started, however, we quickly became overwhelmed in taking on equity and social justice work for an entire library collection at a large research institution. Instead of potentially spending months on a formal plan, we looked for faster, yet deliberate, ways to create change that was long overdue. In response, CDIG's first two years focused on automating purchases of diversity award-winning books, integrating inclusive collecting into daily work and services, updating collection policies for equity and inclusivity, and advocating for equitable and anti-racist collections on campus.

Literature Review

The literature offers numerous reasons why academic librarians should engage in collections-related diversity and inclusion work. Most broadly, the

DOI: 10.4324/9781003167174-9

values and ethics of librarianship, such as those outlined in the American Library Association's (2019) *Core Values of Librarianship*, include access, diversity, service, and social responsibility, placing librarians "in opposition to ... systems of oppression and privilege" (Baildon et al., 2017, p. 7; also see Berthoud & Finn, 2019). This has not always been the case, though, and, more often than not, academic libraries have collected and disseminated resources by White, Eurocentric, male-identified authors (Alexander, 2013; Berthoud & Finn, 2019; Pashia, 2019; Rapchak, 2019). Academic librarians, then, have played a key role in defining the "scholarly record" as consisting primarily of the works of "great White men," and, in accepting this reality, must work toward building a more diverse and equitable scholarly record moving forward (Berthoud & Finn, 2019, p. 165; Morales et al., 2014, pp. 445–446).

In trying to build more diverse and inclusive collections, the literature indicates that relying on vendors and demand-driven acquisitions (DDA) is not enough, as they often perpetuate systemic bias toward historically underrepresented populations (Baildon et al., 2017; Blume, 2019; Kristick, 2020; Morales et al., 2014). In addition to relying on a homogeneous scholarly publishing model, vendors and DDA perpetuate systemic bias via continued use of problematic library classification systems, such as that of the Library of Congress (LC). Evaluation of these systems, including terminology used, has shown that they typically other non-White and LGBTQ+ populations (as well as individuals with different/dis-abilities); this provides a negative, or even damaging, experience for readers who identify as such and makes diverse materials difficult to find (Adler, 2017; Matheson et al., 2020; Nowak & Mitchell, 2016). Another way librarians can engage in collections-related diversity and inclusion work, then, is to counter these classification systems, such as by using more inclusive terminology, creating their own collections focusing on marginalized voices, or creating new organizational schemes (Adler, 2017; Matheson et al., 2020; Nowak & Mitchell, 2016).

Beyond filling gaps in the collection due to problems within the field, academic libraries, specifically, should build more inclusive collections in order to address the needs of students identifying as members of historically underrepresented populations. For instance, Alexander (2013) and Roy (2019) argued the need for building collections to support Native American or Indigenous studies, primarily to better serve Native American students and communities seeking information about their identities or marginalized historical perspectives. Similarly, Matheson et al. (2020) and Todorinova and Ortiz-Myers (2019) highlighted the need for targeted collections and services for students identifying as LGBTQ+. Todorinova and Ortiz-Myers (2019) pointed out that students may prefer the privacy an academic library offers when seeking information about LGBTQ+ topics over visiting a campus LGBTQ+ resource center. Overall, building inclusive collections more accurately diversifies the scholarly record and supports students who want to learn more about their own identities.

In addition to the suggestions highlighted above, the literature provides several recommendations for how librarians can engage in building more diverse and inclusive collections. Recommendations include reviewing vendor relationships, business decisions (including DDA services), or collection policies, as well as purchasing materials from alternative providers and small publishers (Baildon et al., 2017; Berthoud & Finn, 2019; Blume, 2019; Cruz, 2019; Kristick, 2020; Roy, 2019). Libraries may also want to track spending on diverse materials or request additional funding for purchasing diverse materials to ensure the library is honoring its commitment to building inclusive collections (Cruz, 2019). A designated committee, or hired professionals, can evaluate collections for coverage of diverse areas and authors, and build more diverse collections in general (Blume, 2019; Cruz, 2019; Kristick, 2020; Proctor, 2020). Or, instead of creating a separate process via committee, libraries could create diversity and accessibility selection criteria that all librarians responsible for collection development must apply when selecting materials (Baildon et al., 2017; Cruz, 2019). Similarly, librarians could apply new methods for collecting (for example, see Berthoud & Finn, 2019, for their descriptions of spiral and expansive scope collecting); new methods could include involving students or partnering with student organizations, affinity centers, or other related offices on campus (Baildon et al., 2017; Clarke, 2019; Cruz, 2019). Finally, in addition to purchasing diverse materials, libraries should promote them, such as by showcasing works by underrepresented authors or by grouping and tagging works focused on marginalized identities (Baildon et al., 2017; Hogan, 2010).

Grassroot Beginnings

The first group that focused on diversity and inclusion at CSU Libraries was the Libraries Committee on Equity and Inclusion, formed in 2017 and initially chaired by Nowak. Prior, individual faculty members conducted inclusion work and outreach, but often in the absence of organizational support or structure. The committee became responsible for all major diversity and inclusion work in the Libraries, resulting in scattered projects, primarily focusing on building cultural competency, and often neglecting collections. The committee's primary collections effort had been trying to prevent the cancellation of periodicals that represented diverse, marginalized voices. This effort revealed some of the challenges of diversity and inclusion work in collections, such as how usage and other metrics used to evaluate materials often lead to hegemonic and non-representative collections. For example, the committee had to argue for retaining a periodical focused on Indigenous peoples of the Americas that was placed on the potential cancellations list due to low usage. Given that it was one of the few print periodicals the Libraries owned representing Indigenous peoples, the committee did not consider usage the determining factor, especially since high usage among Indigenous students, staff, and faculty at CSU would be considered low usage among all periodicals due to CSU's demographics. The committee also attempted to display periodicals representing marginalized voices in high-traffic areas to provide additional visibility, but the effort was ultimately found to be incompatible with processing procedures, leaving many inclusive periodicals buried in the stacks. Overall, the committee's efforts regarding collections were scattered and reactive since they were already attempting to address all diversity and inclusion needs across the Libraries.

In early 2019, we attended several webinars and workshops on developing diverse and inclusive collections. In response, Thomas and the collections coordinator realized a clear need for a centralized and concerted effort to increase, integrate, and retain diverse materials at CSU Libraries, and formed CDIG, with Thomas serving as the group's chair. Several prominent strategies emerged from the webinars and workshops we attended, which were highlighted as possible activities for the group when it first formed. These included:

- incorporating diversity and inclusion efforts into the collection development strategic plan;
- changing slip notifications to auto-shipments in GOBI (EBSCO's monographic acquisition tool) for subject areas showing significant gaps regarding diverse works;
- curating book displays on diverse topics or works authored by those holding marginalized identities;
- partnering with key stakeholders (e.g., students, faculty, affinity groups) to curate collaborative book displays;
- developing alternative subject and classification schemas for holdings that have harmful or inaccurate LC subject headings;
- encouraging vendors to provide more diverse and inclusive content, along with identifying relevant small presses and non-commercial publishers; and
- and using alternative metrics beyond age and usage to weed collections to ensure historically marginalized perspectives are not disproportionately affected.

Challenges

Enthusiasm to engage in this work was palpable at CDIG's first meeting in summer of 2019; however, just as present was the uncertainty on where to begin. We did not have the time or the budget to take on every strategy at once, so identifying a starting point would be our first challenge. To identify the area of greatest need, we explored tools to help us analyze the diversity of our collection. One tool was the Gold Rush Content Comparison System, developed by the Colorado Alliance of Research Libraries (CARL). This particular tool allows libraries to load their MARC records and compare their unique holdings to those of other libraries within the consortium

(CARL, n.d.). With training, we learned how to use the comparison tool to refine our results by a specific subject heading or LC call number range. For example, we used the tool to compare our unique holdings for the LC call number range E184.5 to E185.98 in an attempt to capture holdings about or written by Black or African Americans. Although the Gold Rush tool is a useful comparison tool for collection analysis overall, we did not find using the LC call number range or subject headings to be an accurate means of identifying works about or authored by individuals with marginalized identities. This is unsurprising given Adler's (2017), Matheson et al.'s (2020), and Nowak and Mitchell's (2016) findings and discussion about the legacy of disenfranchisement and segregation within the LC classification system.

After a failure to obtain useful data via Gold Rush or Alma analytics, we moved toward our own familiarity with the library's collections to identify the area of greatest need. Initial discussions and surface-level evidence, such as our database subscriptions, revealed a few potential areas of focus, including collecting works authored by or about Native Americans or Indigenous peoples of the United States, Black or African Americans, Latinx individuals, or members of the LGBTQ+ community. However, though the webinars and workshops we attended emphasized not trying to include all voices at once, prioritizing our collections efforts by identity simply felt problematic. Our collection suffered from a lack of cohesive representation of marginalized identities, and choosing one to focus on felt like disregarding the needs of others. Facing another roadblock and more time spent on over-planning and over-strategizing, we looked for faster, and more equitable, solutions. Although we knew we had not found a permanent solution, we wanted to make positive contributions to the diversity of our collections sooner than later. We jumped in by focusing on automatic purchase plan conversations with EBSCO's GOBI Library Solutions that were already occurring.

Automating

CSU Libraries has been relying on a print and e-book DDA model since 2012. Though DDA is a useful tool for collection development, librarians now know that it can lead to homogenous or unbalanced collections. Without intervention, DDA can perpetuate systemic bias, cater to a handful of subject areas (or community members), and result in a severe lack of materials on diverse perspectives or by diverse authors (see Baildon et al., 2017; Blume, 2019; Kristick, 2020; Morales et al., 2014).

Being aware of these pitfalls, we explored ways to actively and systematically collect works by and about historically underrepresented groups. As we had recently implemented more automated purchase plans in other areas, such as agriculture, we reached out to our GOBI representative and expressed an interest in adding more diverse materials to our collections. In response, our representative provided us with a list of diversity award-winning titles that we could use to create an automated purchase plan. This list included

74 diversity awards, such as the Asian/Pacific Award for Literature, Black Caucus Literature Awards, Lambda Literary Awards, U.S. Latina/Latino & Chicana/Chicano Literary Awards, and NAACP Image Awards. Due to budget constraints, we were unable to incorporate all 74 awards into our new plan, so we devised specific criteria to refine the list, like removing country-specific awards and selecting awards highlighting the works of historically underrepresented authors. We pared down the list to 37 awards, amounting to roughly 110 books annually. Using the finalized list, our GOBI representative set up a "Diversity Awards Purchase Plan" that began in September 2019 and uses a unique acquisition fund code to help us track expenditures.

Currently, the purchase plan is still operating, with award-winning books continuing to arrive on a rolling basis throughout each year. Additionally, we have taken steps to promote these incoming titles: (1) by creating a book display in the entryway of the main library, a high-traffic area, and (2) by creating custom bookmarks for the books (see Figure 8.1). Each bookmark communicated that the book was a diversity award winner and the Libraries had purchased it as part of an ongoing effort to add marginalized voices and perspectives to our collections. Despite our hope to also make a searchable collection of these titles, our current library system is not well designed for this type of custom labeling, and we have been unable to find a way to mark the books with either a bookplate or note in the online record. However, we are continuing our efforts to promote these books and find a way to create a searchable collection.

When refining the list of awards, we had some concern that selected award categories provided little focus on Native American or Indigenous peoples, women, or people with disabilities. We agreed that a future project to review the purchase plan would be necessary, and in the interim, we explored alternatives for increasing diverse content within our approval plans with GOBI. We selected several interdisciplinary descriptors (e.g., Asian American Studies, Black Studies, Chicano/Hispanic Studies, Disability Studies, LGBTQ Studies, Indigenous Studies, Native American Studies, Women's Studies) and worked with GOBI to retroactively audit our approval plans, for titles published 2018 to late 2019. The audit identified 24,000 titles on our approval plans that matched at least one of the identified interdisciplinary descriptors and had not been purchased. Although it was not fiscally feasible to purchase all titles, we hope to use these data in future to help identify gaps in our collection. Moving forward, we would like to better integrate these interdisciplinary descriptors and other enhanced metadata into our acquisitions workflows to improve our efforts to expand our diverse holdings.

Integrating

As we automated some purchases, we also took steps to encourage student involvement and ownership in the Libraries' collections by integrating inclusive collecting into other work, such as instruction. For example,

Figure 8.1 Custom Bookmark for Diversity Award-Winning Books

in summer 2019, the Libraries' Undergraduate Outreach Group (UOG, including Nowak and Thomas) conducted a grant-funded information literacy instruction program for incoming first-generation students, many of whom were students of color, as part of CSU's Bridge Scholars program. The program's purpose was to support student success, and to help students define success for themselves while making a successful transition to academic research. As part of the program, the UOG encouraged students to consider which voices were missing from academic and scholarly discourse, and which voices they would like to see represented in libraries and other academic spaces. Toward the end of the program, the UOG asked each student to identify a book for the Libraries to purchase, with recommendations being provided via an anonymous form. Idea-generating lists, such as anti-racist or student success reading lists, were provided, and students were taught how to identify books in the Libraries' catalog. The UOG reserved a large portion of the grant funding to purchase the books recommended, and all recommended books were purchased.

There were significant successes and challenges for this activity. Students seemed excited to select books that would actually be purchased, and they made excellent recommendations. Since few restrictions were provided, many students chose their favorite book (fiction, graphic novel, or poetry), a book that represented an identity they held, or book they needed for a course. The UOG considered all of these as serving a purpose in making the collection more inclusive (e.g., purchasing textbooks can decrease students' financial burdens). The process of selecting books seemed to humanize the library for the students, as well as provide a sense of ownership for the Libraries' collection. A major challenge for the activity was students selecting books the Libraries already owned. The UOG encouraged students to search for titles prior to selection, but many students had trouble navigating our catalog. As a result, they were only able to spend a portion of the available funding on students' direct requests. Remaining funds were spent on categories in which students expressed interest (e.g., comics, poetry), with exact titles selected by the UOG.

The UOG was able to include a bookplate in each student-selected book, marking them as chosen by the 2019 Bridge cohort (without naming specific individuals). They also created a coordinating book display, with books on the display being quickly checked out. Books were promoted again at a follow-up pizza party with the students in November 2019. The 2020 Bridge cohort experienced a revised version of the activity, in which students simply recommended books with less focus on pre-searching and using the library catalog. The UOG plans to continue the activity with future Bridge cohorts, with more focus on discussing missing voices in academic spaces and student ownership of the library's collection.

Updating

LGBTQ+ Collection

Before the creation of CDIG, Nowak had already begun updating the Libraries' LGBTQ+ collection over the past few years as part of organizing Pride Month book displays from May to June. The Libraries' print books related to LGBTQ+ topics were badly out-of-date (for example, in 2016, the majority were from the 1980s and 1990s), so updating the collection was a necessity before creating the display. Luckily, book display organizers are granted a small amount of money for the purchase of new books at CSU Libraries, allowing the displays to serve as an opportunity to both update and promote the Libraries' collections. Despite Nowak's efforts, the timing of the display (just as many students were leaving the campus for summer) allowed little engagement.

In early 2020, we were granted additional funding for purchasing materials to improve our LGBTQ+ collections as a project for a temporary, part-time librarian position. The part-time librarian was assigned the task of creating a list of purchase recommendations related to LGBTQ+ topics. CSU Libraries was closed to the public due to the COVID-19 pandemic in the middle of this assignment, so we purchased books primarily in electronic format. As a result, we created a virtual Pride, or Rainbow Book Month, display on the Libraries' website for June 2020 (see Figure 8.2), rather than an in-person display as had been organized in the past. Views for the display were low (fewer than 20), but we are hopeful for increased engagement in future as our patrons become more used to seeing virtual book displays on our website.

Figure 8.2 Rainbow Book Month Virtual Display

Curriculum Collection

In addition to updating our collection on LGBTQ+ topics, we have also begun updating our curriculum collection with a diversity and inclusion lens. The curriculum collection was originally purposed to support the English Education concentration under the English major at CSU and has been mostly limited to books written for children in grades eight through twelve. However, anecdotal evidence from CSU Libraries' Help Desk and librarians has indicated that CSU community members seek picture books and other early children's literature at CSU Libraries. Both Watson and Thomas took on new responsibilities in the summer of 2020 that allowed them to respond to this information need, along with pursuing CDIG's goal of building diverse and inclusive collections. Watson was designated as the liaison overseeing the curriculum and current awareness collections in June 2020 following a retirement, and, shortly after, Thomas was charged with managing the 2020–2021 state grant to libraries, provided to CSU Libraries annually by the Colorado Department of Education. These events coincided to provide Watson and Thomas the opportunity to collaboratively update the curriculum collection.

The curriculum collection policy update (pending final approval; shown in Figure 8.3) focused on expanding the collection's purpose to teaching CSU's Principles of Community—inclusion, integrity, respect, service, and social justice (CSU Office of the Vice President for Diversity, 2021)—in addition to reading and writing, to children in grades pre-kindergarten through twelve. This policy change, along with the state grant to libraries, allowed Watson and Thomas to purchase approximately 250 children's and young adult books that were written by diverse authors and/or addressed diversity and inclusion topics. Titles were selected from GOBI's 2020 Children's Award Finalists spotlight list, the Cooperative Children's Book Center's (CBCC) 2020 Choices Reading List, the United States Board on Books for Young People's (USBBY, 2021) Outstanding International Books List, Indiana University Bloomington Education Library's (2021) "Contemporary Picture Books about Children and Families of Color & Disabilities" list, *New York Times* children's books lists, National Public Radio (NPR) book lists, and anti-racist children's literature lists discovered online. Understanding the power of authentic representation of People of Color in children's literature, Thomas also drew from her lived experience as a Black mother of young biracial children in selecting books that value racial diversity.

In future, we plan to use these lists, along with others like ALA Rainbow Round Table's Rainbow Book List and related bibliographies, to begin assessing the curriculum collection for gaps and continue purchasing relevant titles. In time, we hope to build a robust, and diverse, collection of children's and young adult literature for, and in collaboration with, our patrons.

~~Curriculum Materials~~ **Juvenile Reading** Collection

Purpose

The ~~Curriculum Materials Collection (CMC)~~ Juvenile Reading Collection, maintained in a separate location within Morgan Library, supports the teaching ~~related activities of the Department of English~~ and learning of reading and writing in grades PreK-12, as well as the teaching of CSU's Principles of Community to children in grades PreK-12. The collection supports courses focusing on children's and adolescents' literacy, such as those included in the English Education concentration in the Department of English, Education (General), and Human Development and Family Studies. The collection also supports CSU community members with children and/or with interest in children's or adolescent/young adult (YA) literature. ~~One of the concentrations in the English major is English Education. The English education concentration provides students with preparation for teaching in secondary schools. In addition to the common requirements for the English major, students pursuing teaching licensure take several extra courses in English, as well as education classes through the School of Education.~~

~~Students are required to take E 405 Adolescents' Literature, E322 English Language for Teachers I, E323 English Language for Teachers II, E401 Teaching Reading, E402 Teaching Writing, and ED463 Methods in Teaching Language Arts; the CMC supports all of these courses by providing examples of textbooks, grammars, literature, anthologies, and non-fiction reading materials that assist in the teaching of reading and writing.~~

The processing, maintenance, and circulation of the materials within the ~~CMC~~ Juvenile Reading Collection is the responsibility of CSU Libraries ~~the Library~~, and they are governed by the Libraries' collection management procedures and circulation policies.

Scope of coverage

Literature, anthologies, fiction, non-fiction, textbooks, and other relevant genres that assist in the teaching and learning of reading and writing, or of CSU's Principles of Community, will be collected. Children's books will be selected based on their status as classic or popular works, along with those identified as promoting inclusion, integrity, respect, service, and social justice. Adolescent literature materials will be collected based on lists of the best books for young adults, along with their identification as readings promoting inclusion, integrity, respect, service, and social justice; these lists of best books include: ALA Rainbow Book List, Alex Awards, Best Books for Young Adults, Coretta Scott King Award, Great Graphic Novels for Teens, Margaret A. Edwards Award, Michael L. Printz Award, Newbery Award, Odyssey Award, Outstanding Books for the College Bound, Popular Paperbacks for Young Adults, and Quick Picks for Reluctant Young Adult Readers, Randolph Caldecott Medal, USBBY awards, and We Are Kid Lit Collective reading lists, among others~~; and with suggestions by the faculty from the Department of English~~. Relevant suggestions from CSU community members will also be considered for the Juvenile Reading Collection. ~~Materials selected by or for the Department of English are maintained within the CMC indefinitely.~~

Figure 8.3 Sample of Proposed Revisions to Curriculum Materials Collection Policy

A-Z Database List

In collaboration with relevant Libraries department heads, we have proposed changes to CSU Libraries' "A-Z database list" to better highlight resources supporting research on marginalized populations or voices. One proposed change is adding a diversity and inclusion category under which we would group relevant resources for findability, like what CSU Libraries' has done with academic subjects. Another proposal is adding a custom icon to the "records" of applicable databases in our A-Z database list to indicate whether they focus on historically underrepresented groups or perspectives, such as EBSCO's *Ebony Magazine Archive* or Gale's *Indigenous Peoples of North America*. The icon would highlight relevant resources in context for users, such as when browsing through subject-specific database lists or when reviewing LibGuides for research help. These changes demonstrate one-way libraries can update their online services and collections to help patrons find diverse resources, as well as advocate for diversity and social justice in general.

Advocating

Local Events

An essential component of building diverse and inclusive collections is ensuring that key stakeholders (e.g., administration, faculty/staff) are aware of the value that diverse and inclusive collections bring to the university. A unique opportunity to champion the work of CDIG arose in the aftermath of a difficult moment for CSU. In the fall of 2019, the CSU community was shocked when Instagram photos of four White students wearing blackface, accompanied by the caption "Wakanda forevaa" (a disparaging reference to the Marvel *Black Panther* movie), surfaced and gained widespread media attention. CSU students, faculty, and the larger CSU community were outraged and demanded action; however, since the students posted the photo to their personal social media accounts, the university deemed that they had no recourse to take any punitive action (Burke & Walters, 2019).

In the wake of this and other abhorrently racist incidents that had recently transpired on campus, CSU created the Race, Bias and Equity Initiative (RBEI). The objective of this initiative is to "implement actionable plans to address issues of race (and racism), bias, and equity at CSU and to empower all members of our campus community to learn, work, live and recreate in a safe and welcoming environment" (CSU RBEI, 2021). One of the first actions of the RBEI was to request proposals from CSU students, faculty, and staff to identify equity initiatives that could improve CSU. We viewed this call for proposals as a great opportunity to demonstrate the importance of building diverse and inclusive collections. We submitted a proposal requesting funding to purchase, as well as exhibit and promote, select books, journals, and databases that actively incorporate diverse and underrepresented perspectives into the Libraries' collections.

More specifically, we proposed incorporating and showcasing the knowledge, voices, and stories of Black or African American, Asian American, Latinx, and Native American or Indigenous communities by acquiring resources such as Alexander Street's *North American Indian Thought and Culture*, EBSCO's *Ebony Magazine Archive*, and ProQuest's *History Vault* (a variety of primary sources focusing on issues related to immigration, women's studies, slavery, black freedom, and civil rights, and Indigenous peoples). By promoting, marketing, and providing access to these works, we hoped to encourage further integration of these marginalized perspectives into research and course curricula. We also hoped to continue to foster a sense of belonging for our students, faculty, and the larger CSU community of color. Ultimately, our proposal was not selected as one of the projects that RBEI chose to fund; instead, it was sent to the Libraries Administration with the suggestion to incorporate the idea into existing and new initiatives (CSU RBEI, 2021). In summer of 2020, the Libraries Administration provided extra funding to purchase the *Ebony Magazine Archive*, and a corresponding article detailing its unique value to our collection was commissioned for our donor-centered magazine *Stay Connected*. Though we did not fully achieve our desired outcome, submitting the RBEI proposal did accelerate our attempts to advocate for the importance of diverse and inclusive materials in academic library collections.

National Events

In addition to responding to local events via the RBEI, we also felt an urgent need to respond to the continued systemic violence against Black individuals in the United States, underscored by the 2020 murders of Breonna Taylor, George Floyd, Rayshard Brooks, and too many others. Like many institutions in summer 2020, CSU released a public note of solidarity with its Black and African American community, which the CSU Libraries (2020) echoed in a *Black Rams Matter* statement on their website. Following this statement, the Libraries desperately wanted to put words into action, including via CDIG. We explored the efforts of other libraries creating anti-racist reading lists or other materials, such as the University of California Irvine's (2021) "Understanding and Combatting Racism" list. Thomas led the effort to create our "Educate Yourself: Anti-Racist Readings" webpage, designed to encourage the CSU community to actively engage in critical self-reflection and engagement with issues around racism. The list was linked from a scrolling banner on the Libraries' homepage for several months, and is now linked from the CSU Libraries' (2021) *Equity and Social Justice* webpage. The list received positive feedback from CSU students and staff.

As part of this effort, we were able to align with projects and offices across campus, creating an opportunity for greater impact. In late summer 2020, CSU began an initiative called Rams Read, with the idea that the university community would read, discuss, and host events related to a specific book. The first book selected for the program was Claudia Rankine's *Citizen: An American Lyric*, a powerful book exploring themes relating to anti-Black racism and the Black experience. CSU Libraries was able to provide electronic access to the book, which connected us to several campus initiatives. For example, *Citizen* was promptly included in our anti-racist reading list, and the list was featured multiple times in the CSU Office of the Vice President for Diversity's monthly newsletter to help provide equitable access to the book. This project was part of ongoing efforts in general to purchase books recommended by the Office of the Vice President for Diversity, and other campus organizations, to create better connections between our collections and institutional efforts.

Practical Strategies

Based on our experiences, we offer some practical strategies to those just beginning to build diverse and inclusive collections. First, gain buy-in from collections coordinators and library administrators. This is essential: in addition to the obvious financial support needed for new materials, funding may be needed for promoting new materials or for the group's professional development when first beginning. Consider making connections to the university's or library's strategic plans or diversity statements to gain buy-in, if needed, or build on other initiatives on campus (e.g., CSU's Race and Bias Equity Initiative or Rams Read). Advocating for budgetary support *is* a key part of creating equitable and inclusive collections, and it is worth noting that a library's diversity statement means little without corollary financial commitment.

Next, create a short philosophy or scoping statement to help individuals engaging in the work maintain a defined, concerted effort, especially when new projects are being considered. Also, to avoid becoming overwhelmed, find a small starting point, or a place in the library's collections where you can make a difference. For example, while we wholeheartedly support assessing collections for need, we found this to be a challenge as a first step. Few tools easily support assessing collections for diverse or inclusive materials and it is easy to become overwhelmed when faced with assessing an entire collection. Consider assessing one part of your library's collection or exploring anecdotal evidence of a collection gap as a starting point, as we have done with CSU Libraries' curriculum collection. Using vendor-provided diversity-related lists, lists from organizations such as the ALA Rainbow Round Table, and various bibliographies can all provide a starting point for assessing collection gaps or selecting diverse materials to purchase. Since trying CARL's Gold Rush tool, we have identified several other sources of data to help us gauge potential diversity gaps in our collection. These sources include Alma and Primo analytics, as well as CSU researchers' interests indicated by CSU's Institute for Research in the Social Sciences' (2021) network visualization published dissertations and theses, and more. Though these may not be starting points, we offer them as alternative methods for assessing diverse holdings in academic library collections should you prefer to start with assessment at a larger scale.

In addition to scoping and performing small-scale assessments, consider automating recurring purchases of diverse materials, such as we did with diversity award winners. Or, at least, consider reviewing an existing purchase plan or collection policy with an equity and inclusion lens. For instance, if a weeding policy relies on usage as a key criterion, your library may want to revise the policy to exclude this criterion when evaluating diverse materials, or at least more heavily rely on other criteria first. These small starting points can not only help with potential overwhelm regarding *where* to start, but also with having *time* to start—an often-daunting task among academic librarians with numerous responsibilities.

Finally, a key resource for identifying needed materials is your institution's community. Involve students, faculty, staff, and other community members in identifying materials, and listen to patrons who identify as members of historically underrepresented groups. Ensuring community members' voices are heard and helping them feel some ownership of the collection is a worthwhile move toward building an inclusive collection. Consider integrating these processes in other work within the library, such as information literacy instruction. In addition to involving patrons directly, consider collaborating with student affinity centers and relevant offices at your institution. This can not only help you gain insight into your community's needs regarding diverse materials, but it can also serve as a way to promote the diverse materials your library already owns, such as via events or activities held by affinity centers. Promoting the materials purchased is another key part of creating equitable and inclusive collections. Inclusion occurs not only by adding materials by diverse authors but also by helping patrons from marginalized populations see themselves in the library and feel included as potential users of the collection. Collections with diverse materials are not inclusive if the diverse materials are invisible or inaccessible.

Conclusion

Although we encourage librarians new to this work to start small and focus on a few positive changes, we feel we must emphasize that these are only starting points. Inherent bias and racism in library classification systems, the scholarly publishing process, and more require collection librarians to go beyond relying on DDA or automatic purchase plans. As Berthoud and Finn (2019) stated:

> It is not enough simply to buy a few more books with non-white, female, and/or lgbtq+ faces on their covers. Critical reflection leads to inclusive theory that can guide a more holistic and ethical collection development practice ... It is imperative that we ... begin thinking about our approach to building collections, so that they reflect ideals we claim to espouse in the profession.
>
> (p. 165)

Moving forward, collection librarians, along with their libraries, must take larger steps to address inequities in collections, in order to align with the profession's core value of diversity and social responsibility and, more broadly, to take a stand against the racist and oppressive foundations of US society.

References

Adler, M. (2017). Classification along the color line: Excavating racism in the stacks. *Journal of Critical Library and Information Studies, 1*(1). https://doi.org/10.24242/jclis.v1i1.17

Alexander, D. L. (2013). American Indian Studies, multiculturalism, and the academic library. *College & Research Libraries, 74*(1), 60–68. https://doi.org/10.5860/crl-311

American Library Association. (2019). Core values of librarianship. http://www.ala.org/advocacy/intfreedom/corevalues

Baildon, M., Hamlin, D., Jankowski, C., Kauffman, R., Lanigan, J., Miller, M., Venlet, J., & Willer, A. M. (2017). *Creating a social justice mindset: Diversity, inclusion, and social justice in the collections directorate of the MIT Libraries.* Massachusetts Institute of Technology. https://dspace.mit.edu/handle/1721.1/108771

Berthoud, H., & Finn, R. (2019). Bringing social justice behind the scenes: Transforming the work of technical services. *Serials Librarian, 76*(1–4), 162–169. https://doi.org/10.1080/0361526X.2019.1583526

Blume, R. (2019). Balance in demand driven acquisitions: The importance of mindfulness and moderation when utilizing just in time collection development. *Collection Management, 44*(2–4), 105–116. https://doi.org/10.1080/01462679.2019.1593908

Burke, M., & Walters, S. (2019, September 12). *White Colorado State students won't be punished over blackface photo, school says.* NBC News. https://www.nbcnews.com/news/nbcblk/white-colorado-state-students-won-t-be-punished-over-blackface-n1053126

Clarke, M. (2019). Emancipating minds and collections, while challenging the profession. *ALISS Quarterly, 14*(3), 3–5.

Colorado Alliance of Research Libraries. (n.d.). *Gold Rush®.* Retrieved May 1, 2021, from https://www.coalliance.org/software/gold-rush

Colorado State University Institute for Research in the Social Sciences. (2021). *Join the Network.* https://iriss.colostate.edu/join-the-network/

Colorado State University Libraries. (2020). *Black Rams Matter.* http://lib.colostate.edu/black-rams-matter/

Colorado State University Libraries. (2021). *Equity & Social Justice.* https://lib.colostate.edu/about/equity-social-justice

Colorado State University Office of the Vice President for Diversity. (2021). *Principles of Community.* https://diversity.colostate.edu/resources/principles-of-community/

Colorado State University Race, Bias and Equity Initiative. (2021). *Race, Bias and Equity Initiative.* https://racebiasandequityinitiative.colostate.edu/

Cruz, A. M. (2019). Intentional integration of diversity ideals in academic libraries: A literature review. *The Journal of Academic Librarianship, 45*(3), 220–227. https://doi.org/10.1016/j.acalib.2019.02.011

Hogan, K. (2010). "Breaking secrets" in the catalog: Proposing the Black queer studies collection at the University of Texas at Austin. *Progressive Librarian, 34/35,* 50–57.

Indiana University Bloomington Education Library. (2021). *Contemporary Picture Books about Children and Families of Color & Disabilities.* https://libraries.indiana.edu/contemporary-picture-books-about-children

Kristick, L. (2020). Diversity literary awards: A tool for assessing an academic library's collection. *Collection Management, 45*(2), 151–161. https://doi.org/10.1080/01462679.2019.1675209

Matheson, M., Tait, E., & Reynolds, S. (2020). Checking the pulse of LGBTIQ+ inclusion and representation in the academic library: A literature review. *Journal of the Australian Library & Information Association, 69*(1), 31–46. https://doi.org/10.1080/24750158.2019.1686571

Morales, M., Knowles, E. C., & Bourg, C. (2014). Diversity, social justice, and the future of libraries. *Portal: Libraries and the Academy, 14*(3), 439–451. https://doi.org/10.1353/pla.2014.0017.

Nowak, K., & Mitchell, A. J. (2016). Classifying identity: Organizing an LGBT library. *Library Philosophy & Practice,* 1–13.

Pashia, A. (2019). Black Lives Matter in information literacy. *Radical Teacher (Cambridge), 113*(113), 100–102. https://doi.org/10.5195/rt.2019.611

Proctor, J. (2020). Representation in the collection: Assessing coverage of LGBTQ content in an academic library collection. *Collection Management, 45*(3), 223–234. https://doi.org/10.1080/01462679.2019.1708835

Rapchak, M. (2019). That which cannot be named: The absence of race in the framework for information literacy for higher education. *Journal of Radical Librarianship, 5,* 173–196.

Roy, L. (2019). Finding face: Building collections to support indigenous identity. *Collection & Curation, 38*(1), 19–22. https://doi.org/10.1108/CC-08-2017-0032

Todorinova, L., & Ortiz-Myers, M. (2019). The role of the academic library in supporting LGBTQ students: A survey of librarians and library administrators at LGBTQ-friendly colleges and universities. *College & Undergraduate Libraries, 26*(1), 66–87. https://doi.org/10.1080/10691316.2019.1596857

United States Board on Books for Young People. (2021). Outstanding International Books List. Retrieved April 16, 2021, from https://www.usbby.org/outstanding-international-books-list.html

University of California Irvine. (2021). *Understanding and Combating Racism* [OverDrive Collection]. Retrieved April 12, 2021, from https://ucirvinemain.over-drive.com/collection/1086488

9 Creating EDI Internships within the Academic Library

A Case Study

*Sajni Lacey, Taya Jardine,
and Atmaza Chattopadhyay*

Author Biographies + Positionality Statements

Sajni: I am a biracial, cis-gendered, able bodied, settler woman who lives and works as an uninvited settler on the unceded, ancestral, and ongoing territory of the Syilx Okanagan Peoples. I currently work as the Learning and Curriculum Support Librarian (LCSL) at the University of British Columbia Okanagan. I was born, raised, and completed both of my degrees on the traditional lands of the Anishinaabek, Haudenosaunee, Lūnaapéewak, and Attawandaron Peoples.

Taya: I am a Mi'kmaw woman from Natoaganeg First Nation in Mi'kma'ki, now known colonially as Atlantic Canada and raised on the traditional territory of the Nisenan people. I would like to show my gratitude to the Syilx Okanagan People for allowing me to live and learn on their traditional territories during my undergraduate degree at the University of British Columbia Okanagan and to the members of this community who have invited me into their lives. I am writing my contribution from my home territory of Mi'kma'ki and will be continuing my education on the traditional territories of the xʷməθkʷəy̓əm (Musqueam) First Nation at the time of publication.

Atmaza: I am a queer, brown, cis-gender international student who was born in West Bengal, India and raised in Singapore. I am also an uninvited settler and I am currently living, learning, and growing on the unceded, ancestral and traditional territory of the Sylix Okanagan Nation. I am pursuing my undergraduate degree in the Bachelor of Arts at the University of British Columbia's Okanagan (UBCO) campus. In the fall of 2019, I immigrated from Singapore to so-called Canada in order to attain a postsecondary education. This experience and my own varying immigration status have helped me gain a more transnational insight on the social justice, advocacy, and community-centric work that I am interested in.

Overview of the Case Study

This internship was originally run as a pilot project for the 2020–2021 academic year at the UBCO campus Library. One part-time position was proposed to provide a paid opportunity for undergraduate students to support

DOI: 10.4324/9781003167174-10

the existing, developing, and ongoing Equity, Diversity, and Inclusion (EDI) work at the UBCO Library and, where appropriate, lead small projects (Libguides, display development, collection development support, programming, and outreach initiatives) based on their own interests and ideas. The position was not intended for a student to lead the EDI work of the Library, but rather to compensate a student for their time, voice, and labor in contributing to work already happening within the Library related to initiatives, projects, policy development, and working groups. The Library already had a committee that was tasked with the leadership of this work, but was lacking the student perspective, which this pilot project was meant to support. The structure of this internship was based on existing positions at UBCO's Equity and Inclusion Office (EIO), which involved multiple undergraduate student positions that support the EDI work on the campus.

The lead for this pilot and the supervising position was the Learning and Curriculum Support Librarian (LCSL), who was inspired by the work completed by the EIO and their student employees, and was looking for opportunities to incorporate something similar within the Library. Past efforts had been made in the Library to have volunteer student advisory groups, but the desire was to build capacity, and create a more sustainable and financially compensated opportunity for the student voice to be included into the work of the Library, specifically around EDI. With the support of the Chief Librarian and additional partners within the Library, the LCSL applied for funding for one student undergraduate position through a campus grant opportunity called the Equity Enhancement Fund whose aim is to support "... community-based initiatives that enhance equity, diversity, and inclusion at UBC" and was successful in receiving funding in the spring of 2020 (Equity & Inclusion Office, UBC, n.d., para. 1). As will be discussed in more detail below, based on the strength of the candidates who applied to the posting for this position, additional funding was sought and received from the Library to hire two students.

Institutional Context

The University of British Columbia (UBC) consists of two major campuses in Vancouver and Kelowna, British Columbia. UBCO is the smaller campus, with just under 11,000 students, the majority of whom are undergraduate students (UBC, n.d.). UBC has a cross campus Inclusion Action Plan (IAP) (UBC 2019) that is intended to operationalize "the theme of inclusion, and supports the themes of innovation and collaboration in UBC's strategic plan" (UBC, 2018, para. 1). The IAP was utilized heavily to structure the initial funding application in terms of goals and description of the position. After the grant application was successful, an additional institutional document was released titled the Indigenous Strategic Plan (ISP), which is meant to "... advance our vision of becoming a leading university globally in the implementation of Indigenous peoples' human rights. The plan is the university's response to the United Nations Declaration on the Rights of Indigenous Peoples and the National Inquiry into Missing and Murdered Indigenous Women and Girls' Calls for Justice. It is also UBC Vancouver's response to the Truth and Reconciliation Commission's Calls to Action." (UBC, 2020). This document was incorporated into the structure and work of the positions once students were hired in September of 2020.

Drafting, Posting, and Hiring the Posting

The application for the grant required at least two campus partners to sign on to the project. Within the Library there is a Student Learning Hub (SLH) which offers "a range of supports from peers and professionals that include tutoring in math, sciences, languages, and writing, as well as help with study skills and learning strategies" and hires a number of both graduate and undergraduate student staff to support the work within this space (Student Services, UBC Okanagan, n.d., para. 1). The Manager for Writing and Language Learning Supports, and the Manager for Learning Resources for the SLH agreed to be co-applicants on the grant as they work extensively with and supervise undergraduate students within the Library in a number of roles and responsibilities.

These internships were originally planned as in-person positions that would work collaboratively with existing and developing EDI projects within the Library. In addition, the student interns were expected to propose and enact small projects that they would lead with support from the Library in areas that they were passionate about, and that would serve their personal and/or professional goals for the future. These internships were not meant or intended as pipeline initiatives to get students into the library field, but rather to support the EDI work that was already being conducted and developed in the Library. The main purpose of these students' roles was to ensure that not only was the student voice reflected and integrated into this work, but that the students who were providing it were compensated for their time, effort, contributions, and emotional labor.

The LCSL drafted the job posting based on the position description of the student roles within the EIO with feedback from the co-applicants (see Appendix A) and was posted to the student job board. Five students were interviewed for the position on Zoom. The LCSL, the Manager for Writing and Language Learning Supports, and the Manager for Learning Resources participated in the interviews. Students were provided with one interview question and a short presentation topic in advance of the interview. These included:

1   What do you know about the IAP and how it could be applied to support students on this campus and in the Library?

2   In addition, please pitch to us in five minutes or less, an idea that applies an element of the IAP to a program in the Library (such as a book display, a digital display, a social media campaign, program, or something else you come up with!) on an Equity, Diversity, or Inclusion topic of your choice. Please remember that we will be in a remote context for the immediate future and this should be reflected in your pitch!

During the deliberation meeting after these interviews, the selection committee struggled to select just one candidate. In the discussion, there were two top candidates that came with completely different strengths and skill sets that would be valuable to the work of EDI in the Library. It was proposed to ask the Library leadership team for additional funds to hire both students. This funding request was approved and both students were hired (Taya and Atmaza as they will be referred to from this point forward).

What Was the Structure of the Internship?

When the pandemic started, these positions needed to move online, and as a result, the structure of the internships shifted slightly. The original objectives of these positions were the following:

Completion of a minimum of one to two discrete projects per term, or two to three large projects completed over the academic year, which could include, but are not limited to the following as they apply to historically, persistently, and systemically marginalized groups within the UBC community:

- Collection development gap analysis and/or title suggestions;
- Program(s) aimed at a student population, faculty, staff, or campus partners utilizing Library resources;
- Book or resource displays;
- Co-development and/or facilitation of workshops in the Library or SLH;
- Creation of LibGuides to increase resource awareness;
- Creation of materials and reports that would provide an opportunity for sustainable use of student projects and work going forward (with appropriate credit given), including identified areas for future development;
- Sitting as a student representative on the Library's Diversity and Inclusion Standing Committee.

The basic principles of these objectives remained the same with the move to online, but a heavier focus was placed on project ideas that could be executed via digital platforms, such as social media campaigns, or remote programming. In addition, the Library Equity, Diversity, and Inclusion Committee (LEDIC) had begun work to review and implement aspects of the ISP and IAP. There were several additional library working groups that were initiated during the time of the internships that Taya and Atmaza participated in including an ISP working group, a Learning, Research, and Engagement Working Group, a Summer Anti-Racism Book Club Planning Committee, and a Dismantling White Supremacy in our Library Working Group.

In addition, there were also five goals developed that were used to structure the work of the internships, which included:

- Increasing the student perspective on EDI in the Library;
- Increasing the library's capacity for EDI work within the Library;
- Act on the IAP and the ISP;
- Enable opportunities for the student intern(s) to support their personal, learning, and professional goals;
- Provide an additional paid opportunity within the Library for undergraduate students.

Onboarding and Orientation

The internships started with a two-week training program developed with the co-applicants. This included meeting with the Manager of the Writing and Language Learning supports, the coordinator of the SLH, the Marketing and Communications Coordinator, and the LEDIC. Additional time in the first two weeks was allocated to review the ISP, IAP, LEDIC documentation, the Library's social media account activity, and setting some personal and professional goals for the internship. The LSCL curated a list of supporting readings that the students were required to read and discuss with the supervising librarian in order to structure the context of EDI in academic libraries and the work being done with the Library related to EDI. These included:

- Hathcock, A. (2015). White librarianship in blackface: Diversity initiatives in LIS. *In the Library with the Lead Pipe.* http://www.inthelibrary-withtheleadpipe.org/2015/lis-diversity/
- Morales, M., Knowles, E. C., & Bourg, C. (2014). Diversity, social justice, and the future of libraries. *portal: Libraries and the Academy, 14*(3), 439–451. https://doi.org/10.1353/pla.2014.0017
- Switzer, A. T. (2008). Redefining diversity: Creating an inclusive academic library through diversity initiatives. *College & Undergraduate Libraries, 15*(3), 280–300. https://doi.org/10.1080/10691310802258182

Projects of the Internship

Taya and Atmaza proposed and contributed to a number of projects over the eight months they worked in the Library. An initial project was provided to get the students started. This included a Queer Recommends social media campaign where the Library asked their social media followers on Twitter, Facebook, and Instagram for recommendations about queer stories, which was connected to the EIO's Queer Orientation Programming in the fall of 2020 (see further details here). The students would keep track of the suggestions, post links to materials if they already existed in the Library collection, and support communication that went out via the social media channels about titles purchased via these recommendations (see Figure 9.1).

Throughout the internship, there were a number of other projects completed. The most significant of which was an Authors in Conversation event that hosted two Indigenous authors via Zoom to share some of their work, and then participate in a moderated conversation with Taya and each other about their publications and writing process. This was a collaboration that Taya and Atmaza initiated with the Student Union and the EIO. Taya and Atmaza took the lead in coordinating most of this project including liaising with the authors, developing the questions for the event, developing promotions and communications, attending meetings with the Student Union and the EIO. The supervising librarian was responsible for navigating the licensing contracts for the authors to have the recording of the presentation made available via the institutional repository, and navigating the financial components of the events. The supervising librarian also attended all of the planning meetings with authors, campus partners, and faculty stakeholders, and supported students in the preparation and planning for the event and these meetings.

Figure 9.1 Image from Queer Recommends Social Media Campaign

Source: Dania Tomlinson, Marketing and Communications Specialist, University of British Columbia Okanagan, Library.

Additional small projects that were completed were several libguides for our OutWeek, Muslim Literature Appreciation, Black History Month, and current work is being done on a Syilx Okanagan Peoples Research Guide, and an Indigenous Citation Guide. One of our interns was also able to participate on a librarian hiring committee for a new Indigenous Initiatives Librarian position.

Taya's Reflection

General Internship Organization

I was initially drawn to the EDI internship position in the summer before the fifth and final year of my BA because, as an Indigenous woman engaged in student advocacy throughout my degree, I was curious as to how I could further my passion for advocacy in an institutional space. Like many other students, I began my internship with a vague knowledge of the Library structures beyond the stacks and our institutional search engine, but this program has shown the many ways that Library structures and practices can influence staff, faculty and university higher-ups as well as students. My proposed goals for the internship were to uplift the stories of Indigenous people within UBCO's Library, specifically those told by and for Two-Spirit and Queer Indigenous people. This goal would later be collaboratively built into our major project for term one.

Another draw of the internship was the flexible nature discussed in the interview. Working remotely aided in the team's ability to accommodate working across time zones, this also allowed for Atmaza and me as students to pick up hours and complete tasks as they fit into our schedules rather than during a strict 9–5 workday. The flexible student-driven approach allowed me to balance my busy course load, family and community obligations, and our major projects throughout the year. Although flexibility was core to the success of these positions, I believe the strong lines of communication were further integral to our success as a team. Having open communication not only with Sajni but also with Atmaza from the beginning eased any anxieties around burnout or asking for assistance. In addition to our immediate internship team, Sajni also organized for each of us interns to have a mentor in the Library if any concerns arose.

Authors in Conversation

For the majority of term one, our team developed the Authors in Conversation: Tanchay Redvers and Joshua Whitehead event to be held in the first weeks of term two. The major creative decisions, such as which authors to invite, topics to discuss, and structure of the event were left to Atmaza and me, while Sajni liaised with the wider library bureaucracy regarding issues such as funding and legal. Once it was decided that we would host an event to highlight and celebrate Two-Spirit and Indigiqueer literature, we began to compile a list of Two-Spirit authors with particular attention to folks with recent or upcoming publications. After choosing Redvers and Whitehead, it was my responsibility to contact them with information explaining our proposed event and inviting them to be our honored guests. As a student who will soon be entering the workforce, it was a great opportunity to hone my professional communication skills through our email correspondence with both authors and their management. Through the series of meetings that followed, I was able to gain the confidence in presenting it took to accept the invitation to moderate the event.

The event was structured to have two segments, one which was open to all attendees and a smaller segment that was dedicated to Indigenous participants sharing stories with the authors on a more intimate community level. While the open segment was the most widely publicized aspect of the event, it was always clear among our team that the small group was the most important aspect of growing a strong reciprocal relationship between the Indigenous community and the Library. It was also important to the development of the event that we made connections with Indigenous students on campus through the Indigenous Student Council, Indigenous studies faculty and Aboriginal Programs and Services. Coming into a space that is historically oppressive to Indigenous people, it was important to me that each aspect of the event from the marketing to the discussion questions was informed not only by my own personal experience but also by other Indigenous folks on campus and in the community. Through collaboration with friends and fellow students, we were able to curate questions that engaged Indigenous participants thoughtfully and respectfully. As someone who does not regularly produce poetry and narrative writing forms, I felt drawn to connect with Indigenous student poets and artists in the community to produce questions that young Indigenous artists would find most engaging and helpful to hear answers to from our guests. A close friend and Oji-Cree poet and artist Ashleigh Giffen asked: What changes would you like to see in how "Canadian Literature" engages with Indigenous writers and Indigenous writing methodologies? During the event, we also encouraged questions from the Two-Spirit and Indigiqueer audience members. This portion of our event opened conversation beyond the written word of Two-Spirit and Indigiqueer literature to highlight the advocacy work that comes with the territory: What advice would you give to Indigenous youth involved in advocacy work and how would- how can one balance the responsibility to community with your responsibility to self while navigating this type of work?

It was truly an honor and a wonderful learning opportunity to develop relationships with the authors in a way not generally found in most student employment positions.

Committees and Final Reflection

In term two, I was able to dedicate more of my time to participating in a variety of committees within the Library, including as a member of the ISP committee and a non-voting student member on the hiring committee for the new position of Indigenous Initiative Librarian, a first in our Library. Having gained confidence in my role during term one, I felt comfortable voicing my opinions not only as a student in a committee of professional staff but also as a Mi'kmaw woman in a space of predominantly white women. Similarly, being the only student on the hiring committee, it was important to me that the experiences I had heard from fellow Indigenous students through my position within the Indigenous Student Council be heard and respected. It is my experience that in order for positions such as these to be successful, the supervisor must put genuine efforts into building a reciprocal relationship with the interns and be outspoken in their support of the interns.

Atmaza's Reflection

Application and Initial Goal Setting

Initially, I was hesitant to apply for this position within the UBCO Library because of my fear surrounding tokenism and the appropriation of EDI centric social justice work by institutions. Stamped with the "minority" status in relation to my race, ethnicity, and sexuality, I had experience being included in other institutional initiatives that were framed around EDI however, only served to further the capitalist interests of the organization. My hesitance also emerged from a place of unfamiliarity with the internal workings and organizations of the Library itself. As only a second-year student at the time of application, I was also not very well versed with the myriad of functions of the Library itself and was unsure about what the work would exactly entail.

However, despite these reservations, there were two key things that drew me to this position. Firstly, the posting specifically focused on the IAP and on the Library's interest in implementing goals stated within this institutional document. This reduced my fears regarding tokenism as EDI was not framed as a vague goal that would be used for virtue-signaling purposes. It was reassuring to see that the Library was using the IAP as a foundational structure to further engage in this work. This also helped me better frame the role and capacity of the position. Secondly, it was inspiring to see a branch of the institution that was not specifically created to do EDI or social justice work, have an interest in engaging in this work through a student perspective. I was elated to see that the Library valued and wanted to further engage in EDI work through the student lens.

Throughout the application process and when I was hired into the position, I focused my goals around supporting and fostering relationships between the Library and other campus community groups who do critical EDI and social justice focused work around the university. Specifically, I wanted to engage with various student groups and clubs through initiatives that were directly derived from the goals as stated in the IAP. As the position enabled me to provide a student perspective, I was interested in drawing in and centering multiple student voices from communities that have been historically marginalized. I wanted to specifically amplify the voices, interests, and needs of queer and racialized students within the library space and aimed to do so by fostering relationships with campus community groups and branches that focused on providing a space for such students in this institution.

Working with Various Campus Community Groups

Prior to my onboarding, the Library was already thinking about and planning initiatives around various events such as Trans Day of Remembrance, Black History Month, OUT week that were hosted by other community groups within the campus. This was extremely helpful for me as I was able to gain a better insight on the Library's role and capacity within such events. This also helped me craft various initiatives and propose collaborations with other community groups. For example, after understanding how to navigate around creating a library guide through LibGuides, I was able to reach out to the Muslim Student's Association (MSA) with a plan on featuring and centering books as recommended by community members. We collaborated on showcasing books written by Muslim women authors through social media and a member of MSA also provided their reviews on the books, which was added to the social media posts and onto the library guide. It was also really interesting and motivating for me to see how easily books that were recommended by the community members could be bought and added to the Okanagan collection through the Library.

During Black History Month, we reached out to the African Caribbean Student Club (ACSC) in order to understand how we could support their programming and find avenues for collaboration. By this time, I was more familiar with the Library's role, which further helped me gain confidence upon our grounds of collaboration with the ACSC. We organized a book giveaway in accordance with the various themes of celebration throughout February and also created a reading list that was widely accessible to everyone at UBCO. It was extremely empowering to work with other student leaders and head various initiatives within a student position. Helping foster these critical relationships also gave me a lot of joy.

However, through this process of collaboration, I became aware of how much the institution's EDI work is done by marginalized folks. The responsibility for making space, addressing the needs, and bringing concerns to leadership through feedback sessions, events, and various other initiatives was mostly done by students, staff, and faculty who belonged to minority groups who have been historically oppressed and marginalized. There were very few white, able-bodied, cisgender, heterosexual men engaging in this work. This deepened by appreciation for the work that was being done within the UBCO Library by the staff who were mostly white, cisgender, and able-bodied women.

Overall Learning and Experience

The EDI Library intern position was a fantastic opportunity for me as an international student who is passionate about social justice and advocacy work. It gave me an enriching insight on how to navigate bureaucratic structures while also not being limited by them. Just like Taya, I was able to gain valuable communication skills that would be essential when I do enter the labor force and pursue a career within the realm of social justice and EDI.

Sajni's Reflection

The conception of these positions really stemmed from my instruction and information literacy work. Previous to applying for the funding for these positions, I had been looking at how to create more space in my instructional sessions for the student voice and autonomy as information creators and consumers. As I am sure many of us who are in instructional positions can relate to, the dearth of knowledge and practice related to critical information literacy, social justice, and advocacy led me to constantly reflect on my role in the classroom and where I could facilitate student learning in a way that decenters my role as the perceived "expert" in classroom spaces (see Accardi et al., 2010; Elmborg, 2006; Hankins & Juárez, 2015; Leung & López-McKnight, 2021; Pagowsky & McElroy, 2016). In addition, my personal and professional reading has focused significantly on the culture, history, and ongoing legacy of white supremacy within the academic library space (Delgado & Stefancic, 2017; hooks, 1994; Leung & López-McKnight, 2021; Schlesselman-Tarango, 2017; Smith et al., 2019). I was interested in finding ways that I could decenter the White lens of librarianship within my areas of influence, power, and impact, and empower the student voice. Juxtaposed to this was the reality that I was the only librarian of color at my Library. My reflection on this led me to think and reflect on how little the students from marginalized groups might see themselves reflected in the people and resources made available through the Library. The Library already had a number of student positions, and there was some excellent work being done by those in these positions to have the student voice reflected in displays and programming, but I wanted to explore what it would mean to fund student positions that give space for them to explore their interests and potentially professional goals related to EDI, social justice, and advocacy. As outlined above, I tried to be very intentional and clear with the students, the grant application, and the leadership in the Library that these positions were not meant to inspire or create a pipeline for new librarians. Instead, the goal was for students to see themselves reflected in what the Library did in terms of services and programs, and that they had some control and say in it.

It is actually quite challenging for me to articulate exactly how much of an impact these positions have had on me personally and professionally, and the overall impact working with Taya and Atmaza has had in the EDI work of the Library. From the Library side of things, having the student perspective on so much of the work during this year changed how we organized our programming, how we promoted events and programming through social media, and what we engaged with across the campus. Both Taya and Atmaza brought a depth of understanding to the student context of our work, and their nuanced contributions have done nothing but move the EDI, anti-racism, and social justice work of the Library forward. Having student-led content on our social media platforms, such as through our Queer Recommends campaign, Muslim Literature Appreciation, and Black History Month developed relationships with student groups on campus, as well as opened a dialogue and collaboration with those student groups through our social media platforms, I believe helped students see the Library as being responsive, and reflective of their efforts and work on campus. This relationship building with student groups on campus could not have been done to this level without Taya and Atmaza. Atmaza had incredible connections to a number of student groups on campus, and took the initiative multiple times to reach out to folks and see what we could support through the Library. Taya was on the Indigenous Student Council and worked closely with the campus's Aboriginal Programs and Services, and was able to provide a frank and honest perspective on the needs of those students. This resulted in multiple social media campaigns, which we would have done potentially in some capacity, but unlikely as collaboratively.

On a personal level, these positions have been a breath of fresh air. It has been nothing short of a joy to work with two such passionate students and be able to pay them for their labor and time. Many of the initiatives started by Taya and Atmaza will live on. What I can say was one of the most significant impacts of these roles was having both of them at the table for our EDI committee and the subsequent working groups that branch off of that. Taya and Atmaza, once they had time to see how these groups worked, who was involved, and that I would back them up, gained the confidence to speak up frequently and often. Their contributions helped inform the first iterations of the Library's implementation plan for the ISP, how to structure focus group conversations with student employees for feedback on the Library, how to engage with student groups as campus partners, and just the general perception of the work that is being done in the Library from the student perspective. So going forward, having a paid opportunity for the student voice at ideally all tables to me seems like a necessity within the decision-making structure of the Library.

Lastly, one of the biggest takeaways for me from this work is that I did not think as big as the students did. The concept of the Authors in Conversation event was all them. They worked together on the idea, and made it come to life. When I initially conceived of this idea, I was thinking of mostly small-scale projects, maybe a small targeted event in the Library. The move to online created more space and opportunity for this kind of project. Not only was the planning, coordinating, and execution of this event a success but it was also so energizing to see how much enthusiasm the students had for the work. My role in this event was to navigate the bureaucratic structure of the university such as coordinating the finances, and support the communication and liaising with the author's managers, and campus partners. I provided feedback and support at each step of the process, but they led and initiated all aspects of this event.

Aspects to Continue

There were several aspects of these internships that during an end-of-year debrief meeting were described as essential components of these internships should they go forward. These included maintaining student autonomy in project development, collaboration, and outreach opportunities. In addition, having an established spot on the Library's EDI Committee with the opportunity to participate in additional working groups. Ensuring that there are some initial projects for students to work on when they first start in order to dive right into work. With being remote, there was an extra level of flexibility in terms of work time as students were in different time zones, but this can be maintained going forward, even when we return to campus enabling students to engage primarily online could be a significant benefit.

Changes Based on Intern Feedback and Supervisor Feedback

In the last few weeks of the internship, the team came together to discuss what worked, what did not, and what should be added to the program for future students. Through this, there were several aspects that are going to be hopefully folded into future internships. The first is having peer mentors for the next interns. Originally, since this was a pilot project, the interns were paired up with librarians who were not students to be their mentors. Having mentors was intended for the students to build relationships with library workers outside of their supervisor who they could bounce ideas off of and/or talk to if they had issues with their supervisor. However, since these mentors were librarians, both interns acknowledged that it was a little uncomfortable to speak with them openly, and since the mentorship had no structure, it did not last through the academic year. Now that we have had one successful cycle of interns, in the future those folks can be peer-mentors, if they would like, to the next set of interns.

Additionally, with being able to participate on multiple Library committees, it was also daunting to start participating in a group that was already well established and deep into the projects and work. Providing a longer runway to this participation is essential. It was decided that providing more documentation at the start including the Terms of Reference, existing and ongoing project details, and meeting with the chairs of the EDI committee with the supervisor before attending EDI committee meetings so they feel more supported is essential. Lastly, it was discussed that having a list and description of past projects, existing campus connections and partnerships, and any additional materials used during these internships for next students would be beneficial.

Next Steps + Conclusion

There are some clear next steps that need to happen in regards to this project and internship. The foremost is making these positions available ongoing. With these positions running this year through funding made available for projects related to equity, the proof of concept has been more than successful and needs to be ongoing. Some of the biggest accomplishments of these positions is the relationship building with campus partners, and this outreach should be expanded and developed in future iterations of these positions. Creating more opportunities for student-driven social media content is additionally something that multiple folks within the Library commented on as a success and building that in as part of the positions in the future should be considered.

References

Accardi, M. T., Drabinski, E., & Kumbier, A. (Eds.). (2010). *Critical library instruction: Theories and methods.* LLC: Library Juice Press.

Delgado, R., & Stefancic, J. (2017). *Critical race theory: An introduction* (3rd ed.). New York University Press.

Equity & Inclusion Office, University of British Columbia. (n.d.). *Equity enhancement fund* https://equity.ubc.ca/resources/equity-enhancement-fund/

Elmborg, J. (2006). Critical information literacy: Implications for instructional practice. *The Journal of Academic Librarianship, 32*(2), 192–199. https://doi.org/10.1016/j.acalib.2005.12.004.

Hankins, R., & Juárez, M. (2015). *Where are all the librarians of color? The experiences of people of color in academia.* Library Juice Press.

hooks, b. (1994). *Teaching to transgress: Education as the practice of freedom.* Routledge.

Leung, S. Y., & López-McKnight, J. R. (Eds.). (2021). *Knowledge justice: Disrupting library and information studies through critical race theory.* MIT Press.

Pagowsky, N., & McElroy, K. (Eds.). (2016). *Critical library pedagogy handbook, vols. 1 & 2.* Association of College and Research Libraries.

Schlesselman-Tarango, G. (2017). *Topographic of whiteness: Mapping whiteness in library and information studies.* Library Juice Press.

Smith, T., Tuck, E., & Yang, K. W. (2019). *Indigenous and decolonizing studies in education: Mapping the long view.* Routledge.

Student Services, University of British Columbia. (n.d.). Student learning hub. https://students.ok.ubc.ca/academic-success/learning-hub/

University of British Columbia. (n.d.). Facts & figures. https://ok.ubc.ca/about/facts-and-figures/

University of British Columbia. (2018). Shaping UBC's next strategy. https://strategicplan.ubc.ca/

University of British Columbia. (2019). Inclusion action plan. https://equity.ubc.ca/about/inclusion-action-plan/

University of British Columbia. (2020). Indigenous strategic plan. https://indigenous.ubc.ca/indigenous-engagement/indigenous-strategic-plan/

Appendix A

UBCO Library Equity, Diversity, and Inclusion Student Internship

Job Description:

The University of British Columbia Okanagan Library is working toward creating physical and online spaces, information, and resources that reflect the diverse student community we serve. In this position, the successful candidate will work in collaboration with people in the Library to support, develop, and lead projects that will enact the goals of the UBC Inclusion Action Plan. The student will have the opportunity to support, develop, and lead projects that can include but are not limited to, collection development, display development (books, digital, etc.), programming, outreach initiatives, LibGuides, etc. The goals for this internship are for projects to be developed and completed based on the successful student's interests and professional goals beyond this internship. The successful student will be provided with a peer-mentor who works within the Library for additional support.

Duties:

The successful student will work closely with the LCSL, Senior Manager of Writing and Language Learning Services for the Student Learning Hub, and the Marketing and Communications Coordinator to support, develop, and lead projects that enact the goals of the Inclusion Action Plan for the Library context. The successful student will also be an active member of the UBCO Library Equity, Diversity, and Inclusion Committee to provide the student perspective. The successful student will also work where appropriate with the EIO and their student staff to collaborate on campus-wide initiatives.

Specifically, the student(s) will:

1 Lead and assist with planning and implementing EDI initiatives in the library and on campus including but not limited to collection development, display development (books, digital, etc.), programming, outreach initiatives, LibGuides, etc.

2 Participate in the Library's Equity, Diversity, and Inclusion Committee to provide a student perspective, and contribute to discussion and actions that come from that committee.
3 Assist the LCSL, Senior Manager of the Writing and Language Learning Services for the Student Learning Hub, and the Marketing and Communications Coordinator to support, develop, and lead projects that enact the goals of the Inclusion Action Plan for the Library context.
4 Complete other related tasks and professional development as needed.

Supervision Received:

The successful student will work in collaboration with the LCSL to develop learning goals, work plan, project ideas, and professional development goals. Regular feedback and ongoing support will be provided. The student will be encouraged to self-reflect throughout the internship; will receive mentoring and supervision from the LCSL and the peer-mentor; and will be given a mid-point review and a final review at the end of the internship.

An open and diverse community fosters the inclusion of voices that have been underrepresented or discouraged. We encourage applications from marginalized people on any grounds under the B.C. Human Rights Code, including sex, sexual orientation, gender identity or expression, racialization, disability, political belief, religion, marital or family status, age, and/or status as a First Nation, Metis, Inuit, or Indigenous person.

Please ensure you email a cover letter and resume to sajni.lacey@ubc.ca

September 7th 2020–April 31st 2021, 8–10 hours/week*

*Hours can be adjusted to accommodate the student's abilities and availability.

Required Qualifications:

*   Current undergraduate student-status in any discipline/program of study at UBC Okanagan
*   Must have commitment, and ideally experience with social justice initiatives (such as work with LGBT2SQIA+ rights, Indigenous rights, anti-racism, disability activism, etc.)
*   Demonstrate experience and/or abilities with

    *   Community outreach
    *   Online media development (social media, digital promotions, etc.)
    *   Presentations and public speaking
    *   Working independently
    *   Initiating projects

*   Preferred personal qualities

    *   Creative
    *   Enthusiastic
    *   Responsible
    *   Excellent attention to detail

10 Creating More Possibilities

Emergent Strategy as a Transformative Self-Care Framework for Library EDIA Work

Stefani Baldivia, Zohra Saulat, and Chrissy Hursh

Introduction

Finding a means of self-care as a library professional in institutions of higher education is challenging. Furthermore, because institutions of higher education have been designed for the success of white, ethnically European, cisgendered, abled-bodied, heteronormative men, working in academia if you do not identify in these ways can be an isolating experience (Hathcock, 2015). Self-care becomes an imperative, especially for library professionals who strive to create more just and inclusive environments. To address the challenges of workplace isolation while caring for oneself, Black, Indigenous, People of Color (BIPOC) and white allies are establishing mutual self-care networks within the library and information science profession. Cultivating authentic and liberating relationships in order to transform communities is the work that writer and social justice facilitator adrienne maree brown calls us to do in her book, *Emergent Strategy: Shaping Change, Changing Worlds*. Critical race theory scholars have utilized brown's emergent strategy framework in their appeal for race-radical library instruction, validating the experiential knowledge of students of color in a classroom environment (Leung & López-McKnight, 2020). brown's emergent strategy inspired us to reapproach library diversity work with an emphasis on self-care. For the purposes of this chapter, we define "diversity" work, or equity, diversity, inclusion, and accessibility (EDIA) work, as formal and informal efforts to dismantle white supremacy and combat racism.

This chapter presents our efforts to incorporate tenets of emergent strategy as we work to shape positive change in our libraries and in our communities. We initially explored the use of emergent strategy in the context of institutional change, but quickly recognized the power of its application in transformative self-care. We transitioned from using emergent strategy solely within the sphere of institutional diversity committees to practicing it within communities of care. This chapter begins with discussing the ineffectiveness of formal diversity committees operating within static institutions and also offers an exploration of transformative self-care for library professionals. We then illustrate the elements of emergent strategy by sharing

DOI: 10.4324/9781003167174-11

the setbacks and growth we experienced on a library diversity committee. Our practical application of emergent strategy can be a salve to allay the trauma, anxieties, and disappointments that arise when engaging in diversity work. We cannot depend on institutions to take care of us, so we insist on taking care of ourselves and each other.

The Big 'C' Diversity Committee

The strong undercurrent of institutional whiteness within librarianship and higher education at large makes academic library diversity committee work fraught (Galvan, 2015). The most recent, and often cited, data gathered by the American Library Association shows less than 15% of professionals working in libraries and archives identify as African American, Asian/ Pacific Islander, Latino, or two or more races and ethnicities (2012). Critical race theory library scholars have argued that the liberal, democratic values of neutrality and vocational awe function as a riptide that submerges library workers in a culture of white supremacy (Chiu, et al., 2021). BIPOC and marginalized library workers attempt to swim in an ocean of cultural hegemony, struggling to keep their heads above water.

The difficult position in which diversity workers find ourselves, in "an inescapable double bind - while linking activities to the fundamental, structural overhaul of institutions, often remain financially dependent on them. This becomes relentlessly frustrating as is a gesture simultaneously progressive and co-opted" (West, 1990, p. 94). Counterbalancing this co-optation is the sense of alienation that diversity workers are alone in wanting to address systemic oppression. The responsibility for diversity work is "unevenly distributed" and the efforts of diversity workers are often funneled into the ritual writing of diversity documents (Ahmed, 2012, p. 4). In these instances, Ahmed challenges us to be careful of what diversity documents do, warning us to not fall into the trap of allowing situations where "having a policy becomes a substitute for action ... If what they do depends on how they get taken up, then the action of policy (as law or letter) is unfinished" (2012, p. 11). Whether it be a mission statement, a work plan, a series of goals, or a committee charge, Ahmed concludes that diversity documents can conceal racism (2007).

One manifestation of this obfuscation occurred in summer of 2020, in response to the viral video of the police killing of George Floyd in Minnesota. Institutions of higher education rushed to release statements to express their institutional commitment to social justice and anti-racism. A review of 130 statements found that 60% outlined short-term, performative actions that were "symbolic in scope" and less than 40% identified long-term actions, but failed to articulate assessment strategies for the proposed initiatives (Belay, 2020). Consistent with a critique from critical race library scholars, the majority of institutional statements neglected to explicitly identify whiteness, racism, or account for the different experiences of marginalized racial groups (Belay, 2020; Brown et al., 2021). During these pivotal moments in history, or even during more mundane, everyday activities, diversity workers learn—sometimes in a painful way—who within the organization will speak up about power, inequity, and racism, and who will shut down those conversations.

In an annual survey of academic library leaders, administrators self-reported a stunning increase in their ability to foster EDIA efforts, from 7% in 2019 to 25% in 2020 (Frederick & Wolff-Eisenberg, 2021). This shift is likely attributed to library leaders recognizing the social desirability of expressing support for EDIA work on a self-reported survey. Only the year prior, the same research team reviewed 124 academic library strategic plans utilizing a quantitative text analysis to search for key terms associated with EDIA work (Frederick & Wolff-Eisenberg, 2020). The most frequently appearing term was *diversity*, but neither of the terms *justice* nor *anti-racism* were mentioned in the brief, perhaps demonstrating these concepts did not even merit recognition (Frederick & Wolff-Eisenberg, 2020). The research team was baffled at the mismatch between the library leaders' confidence in EDIA strategies and the absence of the term anti-racist in diversity documents. Critical race theory library scholars would argue that the absence of the concepts of "whiteness" or "race and racism" in academic library diversity documents is conspicuous and normalized in libraries (Brown et al., 2021). Performative diversity work allows library administrators to benefit from talking about equity, without committing to action. Library leaders' "failure to move in this direction furthers inequities and performativity" because administrators set the cultural expectations for their organizations (Ferretti, 2020, p. 142). Library workers are expected to adapt and integrate to these cultural normativity of whiteness (Hathcock, 2015). Institutional, Big 'C', diversity committees are expected to *perform* diversity work, by writing policies or speaking about "diversity, equity, and inclusion" but are not fully supported to execute these policies in order to address the cultural hegemony or dismantle the structural inequities in their libraries.

Research on the low-morale experience for BIPOC academic library workers draws several of these themes together. "Enabling systems specific to minority academic librarians' low-morale experiences include diversity rhetoric, whiteness, white supremacy, and racism" (Kendrick & Damasco, 2019, p. 206). To mitigate the effects of toxic libraries, Kendrick and Damasco point academic library diversity workers toward self-care and self-help strategies. In the absence of institutional change, perhaps we can make biographical changes.

Self-Help, Self-Care, and Transformative Self-Care

The term *self-care* is complex, and means different things to different people. Moore and Estrellado (2018) define self-care as striking a balance between "how much to give and how much to pull back for myself" (p. 379).

Seto et al. (2020) take a multidimensional approach to self-care by defining four dimensions of well-being: affective and psychological, physical, creative, and relational. These multifaceted approaches to self-care are valid, and set a solid starting point for more deeply defining self-care as applied in a professional context.

Social work scholars have produced extensive research on the value of self-care in a professional context. Social work programs place a strong emphasis on building self-care skill sets among employees as a necessary competency to alleviate turnover and burnout. Miller and Grise-Owens (2020) argue for the distinction between *organizational wellness*, defined as "the larger system's role in employee well-being", and *self-care*, which is defined as an individual's efforts to affect their own well-being (p. 6). These are each distinct, but necessarily complementary to address the complex nature of self-care in the workplace, because individual efforts can only go so far. There is a need for "organizations to implement policies, procedures, and programs that promote wellness cultures" and for "supervisors and administrators to model, support, and promote self-care" (Miller & Grise-Owens, 2020, p. 5).

Many public libraries host or hire social service professionals to serve patron needs and these partnerships have led to improvements in how information professionals approach reference services, and the creation of library-specific training for serving patrons in crisis (Westbrook, 2015; Zettervall, 2015). So, social work self-care strategies have been applied in libraries, but the focus is usually on patrons, not library professionals.

A significant portion of the literature that does address the needs of library employees focuses on *self-help activities*, such as taking more breaks, desk exercises to relieve neck tension, or the use of stress balls (Spencer, 2013). Levesque and Skyrme (2019) specify that such self-help activities are most appropriately applied to alleviate simple, day-to-day, low-level stressors. Focusing on these short-term stressors "… does not address workplace stress as the systemic issue it is … Instead, it frames the problem of stress as a personal one …" (Levesque & Skyrme, 2019, p. 9). "The tone of this self-help literature is often cheerful and light, offering simple, practical solutions to complex systemic problems" (Levesque & Skyrme, 2019, p. 9). This approach is strikingly similar to library norms for diversity work. The goal of self-help activities is so that the user can adapt and integrate, but does nothing to change the system of power itself, where "the system in this case is both the nature of the academic library and the university as an institution" (Levesque & Skyrme, 2019, p. 12). The solution for workplace stress, in these cases, is to (1) acclimate to system norms which might mean abandoning efforts at individual self-care altogether, and/or (2) getting away from or avoiding workplace stress either physically or through mental diversions (Levesque & Skyrme, 2019, p. 9). Ultimately, even with the use of these self-help activities, there remains a tendency of the library profession to place responsibility solely on the individual, discounting the organization's role in supporting self-care (Lacey, 2019, p. 5).

Another category of the literature dives a bit deeper into intentional *self-care practices*. Craddock (2019) suggests setting boundaries for work duration and how to "say no" or delegate tasks (p. 13). Oud (2005) speaks to the importance of professional mentorships, since there is an expectation for new library employees to adapt themselves to fit into the existing work environment. But traditional mentorship models are problematic in and of themselves. Inherent power structures overshadow the importance of teaching about culture to new employees (or even recognizing work culture), since participants already in the culture have become accustomed to and unwittingly embedded into the existing system (Lacey, 2019, p. 4).

Another thread of the literature presents a holistic, systematic approach to self-care that speaks to meeting individual needs but also recognizes how institutional culture and societal oppressions impact one's ability to care for self in a professional context. Self-care need not be the onus of the individual accompanied by the expectation to assimilate to workplace norms. Instead, institutions must view self-care with a relational, long-term purpose for change. Self-care can be one of many means to dismantle the systems of oppression that spawn workplace cultures that do not value change and also encourage burnout among library employees.

A positive coping strategy for many women of color is activism. Moore and Estrellado refer to activism as "a necessary force that sustains them in the library profession and is an important part of their core values" (2018, p. 383). This type of self-care, *transformative self-care, looks* similar to other forms of self-care, and can include: meditation and mindfulness, exercise, spending time within a supportive community, and consuming or creating art (Moore & Estrellado, 2018, p. 380). However, Moore and Estrellado (2018) distinguish transformative self-care by the following outcomes:

- replenish self,
- build communities and support systems,
- give and get inspiration from those who came before us,
- reaffirm our intersectional identities and whole selves,
- creating and promoting change agents,
- resist assimilation, and
- validate shared experiences.

Audre Lorde framed the defining characteristics of transformative self-care, broadened from the personal to the political, writing "caring for myself is not self-indulgence, it is self-preservation, and that is an act of political warfare" (Lorde, 2017, p. 61). A former librarian, and a Queer Black woman, Lorde's book, *A Burst of Light* (2017), is in many ways an authentic expression of transformative self-care. Lorde deepens our conceptualization around self-care in several ways, referring to self-conscious living as a life with "vulnerability as armor" (p. 58), empowerment forged through self-scrutiny (p. 28), and active meditation as a form of self-control (p. 38).

The elements of emergent strategy are closely related to Lorde's writings, but emergent strategy is ultimately centered on the core ideologies of transformative self-care as presented by Octavia Butler. Jasmine Noelle Yarish (2021) presents a stunning interpretation of *Parable of the Sower* through the lens of, as she calls it, "an abolitionist politics of self-care" (p. 58). Butler's self-care calls readers to learn from one another and concurrently, stop lying to oneself by practicing authenticity. At the heart of an abolitionist politics of self-care is the "need to embrace reality while simultaneously moving beyond both the status quo of the present and a romanticization of the past" (Yarish, 2021, p. 58). Similar to Lorde, Butler's self-care ideology is a revolutionary project, a means of resistance, and a path to collective liberation (Yarish, 2021, p. 60). However, Butler goes on to define her brand of self-care as "rooted in mutual aid and the celebration of learning through difference" (Yarish, 2021, p. 59) which purposefully goes beyond individual practices toward a collective restructuring (p. 60). As Butler, Yarish, brown, and others see it—transformative self-care takes place as we interact with truth, and as we collectively change as a result of learning new truths. Importantly, this concept is central to Butler's self-care: Be ready for and welcome change, so that we can learn from it and (ultimately) shape it. This hyper-focus on change is somewhat unique to Butler's writings on self-care, and shaping change is also the foundation for brown's emergent strategy.

Emergent Strategy in Practice: Transforming Relationships and Power

In *Emergent Strategy: Shaping Change, Changing Worlds* (2017), brown gifts readers a framework for positive transformation based on her activism in social justice movements, she writes:

> ... emergence notices the way small actions and connections create complex systems, patterns that become ecosystems and societies... it is how we change. Emergent strategy is how we intentionally change in the ways that grow our capacity to embody the just and liberated worlds we long for.
>
> (p. 3)

brown reminds readers repeatedly through the text that small actions build patterns, which cause ripple effects of change. Inevitably, the changes our committee enacted rolled outward to the rest of the library. As library professionals, we did not want our personal self-care practices to enable us to merely survive in unhealthy work environments, we wanted to thrive together. brown writes, "We are brilliant at survival, but brutal at it" (brown, 2017, p. 6). We have found that emergent strategy is a useful lens for transforming relationships and power among library professionals. These intertwined transformations were liberating because they helped us step back to see a wider view of diversity committee work, and also relieved us of the burden of achieving institutional outcomes. The emphasis is on strengthening our connections, to root them in self-preservation and community care. Applying emergent strategy has transformed our interactions with each other, allowing us to create healthy boundaries, avoid performative work, and build community with our library colleagues. To showcase this, we explore each element of emergent strategy in relation to our own experiences as academic library professionals engaging with EDIA work.

Fractals

Three years after its formation, our library's diversity committee hit a period of stagnation. We were limited on resources, people power, and full institutional support to achieve our objectives. Training opportunities were optional, and instead of proper examination into social justice, equity, and power, the diversity committee efforts were reduced to facilitating ice-breaker activities in bi-yearly retreats. Recognizing our struggle to engage our colleagues, the diversity committee retreated and regrouped, slowing down to focus on the patterns that we had allowed to develop. We were burnt out, frustrated with the lack of support for our efforts, hurt and angry that we felt ineffective. Grace Lee Boggs says, "transform yourself to transform the world" (as quoted by brown, 2017, p. 53). We realized the pattern we had engaged in was replicating the abuse and harm we had experienced within our library institution. This is the *fractals* element in motion, connecting the relationship between small and large actions. Fractals occur in nature, but when applied to organizational change, fractals occur when "what we practice at the small scale sets the patterns for the whole system" (brown, 2017, p. 53). We began practicing this new approach among our colleagues, hoping to improve collaboration and communication across library units. In acknowledging the fractal element at play in our libraries, we can disrupt harmful patterns and begin to heal.

Intentional Adaptation

The diversity committee built on this pattern by arranging a virtual workshop with library professional development consultant and EDI coordinator, Elaina Norlin, a researcher on the topic of library worker engagement, we asked her to lead a discussion on library work climate. Norlin's workshop focused on workplace self-esteem, demonstrating the connection between a healthy and positive workplace environment and organizational commitment to social justice and equity. Norlin's analysis mirrors the *intentional adaptation* element of emergent strategy, identifying trust among colleagues as crucial to organizational success (brown, 2017). When it comes to organizational contexts, brown recommends shifting from a culture of strategic planning to focus instead on strategic intentions, encouraging team members to practice internal self-reflection instead of reacting to external changes outside of the group's control. She writes (2017) "the clearer you are as a group about where you're going, the more you can relax into collaborative innovation around how to get there" (p. 70).

Emergent strategy advises us to be intentional with our energy, accepting change with curiosity while staying tethered to purpose. brown also emphasized the importance of adapting toward pleasure, suggesting we lean into what feels good and quickly releasing what isn't helpful (2017, p. 72). The workshop affirmed for the diversity committee that to practice social justice, building healthy, joyful, authentic relationships based on trust was imperative.

Interdependence and Decentralization

One of the authors served as the inaugural diversity committee chair and after nine months of experiencing micro-aggressions, verbal abuse, and continued gas-lighting from a senior administrator, was overwhelmed. The chair stepped back from leadership, to serve instead as an advisor to the committee. Although competition and independence are rewarded in higher education, *interdependence and decentralization* in practice consist of "mutual reliance and shared leadership, vision" (brown, 2017, p. 87). In this element, brown (2017) outlines four iterative steps to working toward interdependence: being seen, being wrong, accepting inner multitudes, and asking for and receiving what one needs. After serving as an advisor to the diversity committee for three more years, the former chair realized a biographical change was necessary. Putting the practice of interdependence and decentralization into action, this individual asked for what they needed and completely stepped away from institutional diversity committee work. The team understood this was not a rejection, but more an affirmation of the collaborative relationships between diversity committee members, which now existed outside the boundaries of the institution. In private correspondence, a colleague offered reassurance, "Just because some of our work isn't conducted through a formal institutional group, it doesn't mean we aren't expending time and labor externally to provide necessary support of POC, in addition to key outcomes for our institutions". Decentralization allows us to practice social justice, with dignity, authenticity, autonomy, at our own pace.

Nonlinear and Iterative

While drafting a library strategic plan, the diversity team led a discussion on whether to incorporate a new strategic goal specifically focused on EDIA efforts. Conversation stalled when library personnel fractured on whether components of the goal should be incorporated throughout the strategic plan or if the goal should stand alone. One individual asserted that no action should be taken to integrate EDIA goals into the library strategic plan, noting that the library already includes diversity in a values statement.

Warned by Ahmed about the harm of performative diversity documents, the diversity committee weighed whether our colleague's critique was genuine. brown (2017) writes "... we put up the critiques to excuse ourselves from getting involved ... to protect our hearts from getting broken ... Critique alone can keep us from having to pick up the responsibility of figuring out solutions" (p. 112). The diversity committee's efforts on the library's strategic plan exemplify the *nonlinear and iterative* element of emergent strategy. Drawing the fractal element forward, brown asserts that growth is not linear, but an iterative process. Emergent strategy invites us to approach the impulse for perfection with a willingness to "make space for the natural order to emerge" (brown, 2017, p. 119). Calling attention to the cultural icon, Rihanna, who has a tattoo that states "Never a failure, always a lesson", brown reminds us that errors, mis-steps, and constructive criticism are all part of the creative experimental process (2017, p. 41).

Resilience

brown defines *resilience* as a response, "unveiled when we are triggered, injured, heartbroken, attacked, challenged" (2017, p. 126). The conversation around strategic planning with library personnel demonstrated to the diversity committee that diversity work was not a priority for senior administration, simply a value to gesture toward. Library and university administration continued to be satisfied with performative diversity work, unwilling to invest in social justice. brown ties the concept of *transformative justice* to the resilience element, clarifying that resilience is necessary to recover from repeated injustice, and the goal of transformative justice is to change those conditions (2017, p. 126). She reminds us to start small, look within and recognize how we may engage in our own harmful behaviors, then create new patterns, which she identifies as liberated relationships (2017, p. 133).

Within *liberated relationships*, community members exercise radical honesty (speak your truth, be authentic, ask for what you really want); acknowledge dynamics (related to gender, class, ability, race, and power); and relinquish Frankenstein (be curious, not controlling) (brown, 2017, p. 143). Committing to practicing liberated relationships, our team developed a better approach on how to communicate and collaborate with one another. This enabled us to embrace the reality of the deteriorating diversity committee experiment, while recognizing the failure was not our burden to carry. Slowly, our committee had transformed into a community of care, free of institutional limitations.

Creating More Possibilities

Creating more possibilities is presented as the final element of emergent strategy, rooted in the Earthseed maxim, "All that you touch you change, All that you change, changes you" (Butler, 1993, as cited by (brown, 2017,

p. 163). brown empowers us to build liberated communities in which we can be mutually reliant on each other and practice repeated vulnerability (2017).

In January 2021, we initiated a virtual monthly meditation meeting and deep reading of *Emergent Strategy* for library professionals, incorporating Octavia Butler's transformative abolitionist politics of self-care. The meditation space and learning community, called Creating More Possibilities, was a forum to collaborate outside the boundaries of a single institution where library workers could engage in liberated relationships, practice radical honesty, be validated when they recognize harmful patterns, and work on establishing new patterns rooted in the principles of emergent strategy. We put the creating more possibilities element into practice with professionals from across the United States, meeting monthly to discuss each element of emergent strategy, to explore the broader application it could serve in libraries.

Conclusion

It is worthy to note that several of these scenarios and discussions occurred during a tumultuous year. While the nation and world react to existential climate change, responding to pandemic life while working from home, we leaned into emergent strategy, an instrumental tool for both professional persistence and self-care practice.

Each of the six elements of adrienne maree brown's emergent strategy serves as a collective lens through which library diversity workers can conceptualize and engage in transformative self-care. Placing institutional responsibility for EDIA initiatives on the shoulders of a few individuals, leads to stagnation and suffocates change. By recognizing fractals, engaging in self-reflection then intentionally adapting, we can dismantle harmful behavior patterns within ourselves and establish new patterns. With interdependence and decentralization, we can shift our concept of power, allowing for leadership to take new forms, for individuals to rise up or fall back when needed. In our observance of patterns, we see how growth occurs in a nonlinear iterative process through trial, error, and adjustment. Within a community of care, we can create more possibilities for transformative change when we share what may hurt or offend us, practicing resilience in the face of injustice. Practicing social justice through an abolitionist community of care results in building authentically supportive relationships, rooted in honesty, wherein individuals are open to change and willing to learn from mistakes.

By transforming our relationships with each other as committee members and colleagues, we embraced each other's humanity, often overlooked in the workplace. We each made mistakes, we had conflict, disagreements, through which we generated a better understanding about ourselves and our approach to library and EDIA work. As we transformed our relationships by applying the elements of emergent strategy, this in turn transformed our view on power. We began our work believing that institutional outcomes would lend power to EDIA work, and found instead that power was more fully felt in the community we built with each other and within ourselves.

References

Ahmed, S. E. (2007). "You end up doing the document rather than doing the doing": Diversity, race equality and the politics of documentation. *Ethnic and Racial Studies, 30*(4), 590–609. https://doi.org/10.1080/01419870701356015.

Ahmed, S. E. (2012). *On being included: Racism and diversity in institutional life.* Duke University Press.

American Library Association. (2012). *Diversity counts.* American Library Association. http://www.ala.org/aboutala/offices/diversity/diversitycounts/2009-2010update

Belay, K. (2020, November 16). *What has higher education promised on anti-racism in 2020 and is it enough?* EAB. https://eab.com/research/expert-insight/strategy/higher-education-promise-anti-racism/

brown, a. m. (2017). *Emergent strategy: Shaping change, changing worlds.* AK Press.

Brown, J., Cline, N., & Mendez-Brady, M. (2021). Leaning on our labor: Whiteness And hierarchies of power. In S. Y. Leung, & J. R. Lopez-McKnight (Eds.), *Knowledge justice: Disrupting library and information studies through critical race theory* (pp. 95–110). The MIT Press.

Chiu, A. Ettarh, F. M., & Ferretti, F. M. (2021). Not the shark, but the water: How neutrality and vocational awe intertwine to uphold white supremacy. In S. Y. Leung, & J. R. Lopez-McKnight (Eds.), *Knowledge justice: Disrupting library and information studies through critical race theory* (pp. 95–110). The MIT Press.

Craddock, I. (2019). Don't sacrifice self-care. *School Library Journal, 65*(7), 13.

Ferretti, J. A. (2020). Building a critical culture: How critical librarianship falls short in the workplace. *Communications in Information Literacy, 14*(1), 134–152. https://doi.org/10.15760/comminfolit.2020.14.1.10.

Frederick, J. K., & Wolff-Eisenberg, C. (2020, May 26). *Measuring what matters: Equity, diversity, inclusion, and accessibility in academic library strategic plans.* Ithaka S+R. https://sr.ithaka.org/blog/measuring-what-matters/

Frederick, J. K., & Wolff-Eisenberg, C. (2021, March 17). *National movements for racial justice and academic library leadership: Results from the Ithaka S+R Library Survey 2021.* Ithaka S+R. https://sr.ithaka.org/publications/national-movements-for-racial-justice-and-academic-library-leadership/

Galvan, A. (2015, June 3). *Soliciting performance, hiding bias: Whiteness and librarianship.* Library Juice Press. https://www.inthelibrarywiththeleadpipe.org/2015/soliciting-performance-hiding-bias-whiteness-and-librarianship/

Hathcock, A. (2015, October 7). *White librarianship in blackface: Diversity initiatives in LIS.* In the Library with the Lead Pipe. http://www.inthelibrarywiththeleadpipe.org/2015/lis-diversity/

Kendrick, K. D., & Damasco, I. T. (2019). Low morale in ethnic and racial minority academic librarians: An experiential study. *Library Trends, 68*(2), 174–212.

Lacey, S. (2019). Job precarity, contract work, and self-care. *Partnership, 14*(1), 1–8. https://doi.org/10.21083/partnership.v14i1.5212

Leung, S. Y., & López-McKnight, J. R. (2020). Dreaming revolutionary futures: Critical race's centrality to ending white supremacy. *Communications in Information Literacy*, *14*(1), 12–26. https://doi.org/10.15760/comminfolit.2020.14.1.2.

Levesque, L., & Skyrme, A. E. (2019). New librarians and the practice of everyday life. *Canadian Journal of Academic Librarianship*, *5*, 1–24. https://doi.org/10.33137/cjal-rcbu.v5.29652

Lorde, A. (2017). *A burst of light: And other essays*. Ixia Press.

Miller, J., & Grise-Owens, E. (2020). Self-care: An imperative. *Social Work (New York)*, *65*(1), 5–9. https://doi.org/10.1093/sw/swz049

Moore, A. A., & Estrellado, J. E. (2018). Identity, activism, self-care, and women of color librarians. In R. L. Chou, & A. Pho (Eds.), *Pushing the margins: Women of color and intersectionality in LIS* (pp. 349–389). Library Juice Press.

Oud, J. (2005). Jumping into the deep end: Training for new academic librarians. *Feliciter (Ottawa)*, *51*(2), 86–88.

Seto, A., Becker, K., & Lau, J. (2021). "When you take this jump and cross racial boundaries": Parents' experiences of raising multiracial children. *The Family Journal (Alexandria, Va.)*, *29*(1), 86–94. https://doi.org/10.1177/1066480720964713.

Spencer, R. M. (2013). Taking care of yourself: Stress and the librarian. *Community & Junior College Libraries*, *19*(1–2), 11–20. https://doi.org/10.1080/02763915.2014.894862.

West, C. (1990). The new cultural politics of difference. *The Humanities as Social Technology. October* (53), 93–109. doi:10.2307/778917

Westbrook, L. (2015). "I'm not a social worker": An information service model for working with patrons in crisis. *The Library Quarterly (Chicago)*, *85*(1), 6–25. https://doi.org/10.1086/679023.

Yarish, J. N. (2021). Seeding a Black feminist future on the horizon of a third reconstruction: The abolitionist politics of self-care in Octavia Butler's *Parable of the Sower. Journal of Women, Politics & Policy*, *42*(1), 58–72. https://doi.org/10.1080/1554477X.2021.1870089.

Zettervall, S. (2015). Whole person librarianship: Best practices focuses on innovative ideas from libraries nationwide. *Public Libraries*, *54*(2), 12–13.

11 Diversity Fatigue

Acknowledging and Moving Beyond Repetitious Emotional Labor

Joy Marie Doan and Rahni B. Kennedy

Introduction

The term "diversity fatigue", once heard and understood, has an instant connection to people, especially those that identify themselves as Black, Indigenous, and People of Color (BIPOC). It summarizes the strenuous work needed to implement diversity, equity, and inclusion (DEI) initiatives. Furthermore, it may begin to describe the overwhelming feelings of being so close to the importance of DEI work while dealing with what seems a continuing resistance against it.

For the past 30 years, strategies such as recruiting and maintaining a diverse workforce, stratifying equal opportunities, and diversifying the terrain have permeated recruitment strategies at cultural heritage institutions, including libraries, museums, and archives. While these efforts have arguably made a positive impact on the percentage of physical representation of BIPOC in these spaces, they have not altered the work culture at the same rate (Blackburn, 2015; Hsu, 2017; Vinopal, 2016). Moreover, recruitment and retention efforts that inadequately address recurrent needs (e.g., equal and unbiased deliberation) of BIPOC employees habitually result in their continued frustration, decreased morale, and, "a loss of trust and respect, as people feel that they are not valued or being rewarded properly" (Fernandez & Davis, 1998, p. 147). In order to retain BIPOC personnel, many institutions are placing a larger emphasis on DEI initiatives (e.g., ASERL DEI recruitment and retention task forces, ACRL Diversity Alliance). While there is a heightened amount of pressure to enhance DEI initiatives in Library and Information Science (LIS), there is conversely an increased burden placed on BIPOC employees to advocate for and initiate such projects. This results in these employees being pulled into conversations, projects, and initiatives that ultimately culminate in an added expenditure of energy not experienced by their non-BIPOC counterparts (Lam, 2018). Diversity fatigue is the added pressure placed on BIPOC to expend their resources and energies. The term was coined in the 1990s by corporate recruitment strategists and was once synonymous with diversity recruitment (Miranda-Wolff, 2019). However, in recent years diversity fatigue has come to be associated with

DOI: 10.4324/9781003167174-12

the disproportionate emotional labor exhibited by BIPOC to further DEI initiatives at their institutions (Blanche, 2018).

Diversity fatigue negatively influences the work experiences of BIPOC library personnel and may result in several negative outcomes for the organization, including, but not limited to; (1) decreased retention of BIPOC personnel, (2) decreased morale at all levels, and (3) heightened cultural intolerance. This chapter aims to address the systemic structure of diversity fatigue and how it influences BIPOC work experiences in LIS (i.e., academic librarianship). Moreover, we address how the expectations surrounding DEI work by BIPOC personnel in these spaces have negative repercussions on these individuals' morale, wellness, and professional growth.

Diversity Fatigue

Though many may automatically associate the term diversity fatigue upon hearing it, agreeing on an all-encompassing definition is actually a task in itself. Diversity fatigue was the term previously used in the corporate world to refer to the work of recruiting personnel from minority groups to create a more diverse workforce and the exhausting work of trying to accomplish that (Hsu, 2017; Miranda-Wolff, 2019). From there, it took on a wider meaning outside the workplace of literally being tired of diversity. (Hsu, 2017). The term evolved over time to include the resistance against political correctness, being overwhelmed with DEI work, and at the same time not really fulfilling it (Miranda-Wolff, 2019). Today diversity fatigue is associated with the time to take on the complex issues that surround DEI in addition to the commitment to continue these initiatives long term (Miranda-Wolff, 2019). In addition, it is hard to stay committed to this work when progress seems to be slow and non-existent (Blanche, 2018). Other terms that could fall under diversity fatigue include, but not limited to, battle fatigue, emotional labor, activist labor, and invisible labor.

With the recent uprisings in social justice issues during the recent global pandemic, the meaning of diversity fatigue has come up more to the surface. Institutions, now more than ever, are looking to BIPOC personnel to guide them and lead the efforts toward DEI initiatives. Evidence that past initiatives were ineffective either because they were not adhering to the interest of underrepresented groups or not coming from a standpoint of being intentional. Conflicting narratives surrounding institutions' official commitment to DEI initiatives coupled with employee resistance to new DEI initiatives indicate needed effort from library administrators in molding positive change in their environments. Library administrators (e.g., deans, directors, department heads) cannot err toward silence or passivity (Wasserman et al., 2008). There is a need for managers to engage in problem-solving, expose them to people from different groups, and to encourage social accountability for change (Dobbin & Kalev, 2016).

Recent research has shown that management's redressing of diversity fatigue leads to positive impacts for the organization, including increased trust and morale among employees, as well as greater efficiency in deliverables (Farmanesh et al., 2020). An example of an academic library that is proactively working to mitigate diversity fatigue is the University of North Carolina at Chapel Hill. The Vice Provost for University Libraries and University Librarian Elaine L. Westbrooks issued a statement shortly after the murder of George Floyd that the libraries needed to engage in the role of reckoning acknowledging that everything is "traditionally centered on whiteness and patriarchy as a default" (Chappell, 2021; UNC Chapel Hill Libraries, 2020, para. 3). Then it becomes a situation where the people who are most close and committed to the work experience the greatest amount of fatigue (Lam, 2018).

Diversity Fatigue within Universities

Universities are not immune to concerns similarly faced by other corporate or non-profit businesses (e.g., ineffective job performance reviews, inefficient training methodologies, lack of equipment and facilities). Moreover, universities have (by and large) recognized a need to address diversity concerns on their campuses for their students, staff, and faculty. Often this takes the form of committees or task forces that focus on the need for respect and understanding of various identities (Hartlep & Ball, 2019; Leon & Williams, 2016). While many universities have well-intentioned diversity initiatives (e.g., recruitment efforts, diversity committees), there is often a chasm between an accepted committee or group charge and unsolicited offers to aid in diversity governance for a department, college, or university. In other words, individuals within any given university agree that there are benefits to having committees or task forces aimed at focusing on diversity, but far less of the same individuals volunteer to be members of said committees. As a result, many BIPOC in academia are encouraged, directed, or appointed to serve on such committees and help their departments, the college, and/or university develop diversity strategies (Nance-Nash, 2020).[1] BIPOC in academia, faced with this situation, find themselves in a Catch-22. The university community is taking a seemingly active commitment toward a more inclusive environment, and, conversely, the same community has created a web of emotional labor–uncompensated time and energy–from which its BIPOC community cannot easily escape.

Diversity fatigue in university settings primarily emerges from the emotional labor BIPOC exerts battling diversity resistance.

> Resistance to change often is rooted in fears about an uncertain future, the relinquishment of the familiarity of a comfortable present, and perhaps frustration over the lack of control one may experience … change is often a reflection of a perceived loss of status, power, and influence.
>
> (Thomas & Plaut, 2008, p. 3)

Thomas and Plaut posit that diversity resistance is an intentional (or, in some cases, unintentional) reluctance to change organizational practices that will yield more opportunities for effective diversity learning. Organizational change in universities often moves at a glacial pace that at the best of times may be met with resistance (e.g., rejection, insubordination, stonewalling). University responses to address its practices, or lack thereof, surrounding diversity have grown exponentially in the last decade. However, it has not necessarily followed that organizational behavior at a micro-level has followed suit.

Change activists, as represented by a diversity committee or task force heralding workplace diversity training and policies may be met with a culture of intolerance and other means of covert resistance that can prove to lower morale and be emotionally debilitating (Lam, 2018; Thomas & Plaut, 2008). Over time the emotional labor experienced by BIPOC serving on diversity committees and task forces at universities may result in long-term behavioral stress patterns associated with activist burnout or diversity fatigue, which namely manifests as an inability for those that are passionate about the committee or task force charge to effectively participate in the group's work (Gorski, 2018).[2] Experienced diversity fatigue coupled with diversity resistance can result in negative, "financial, developmental and emotional costs" for the university that stagnate its strategic goals (Thomas & Plaut, 2008, p. 11). However, scaffolded, cooperative learning that addresses the benefits of a diverse campus may simultaneously assail diversity resistance and diversity fatigue (Thomas & Plaut, 2008).

Diversity Fatigue within Academic Librarianship

Despite being viewed as third safe spaces[3] for students and faculty, the university or college library personnel are not immune from the diversity resistance or fatigue invoked by library diversity committees or task forces (Wexelbaum, 2017). However, on this micro-level, the negative costs of diversity resistance and fatigue may be keenly felt. In the last generation of academic librarians, there has been an emphasis on recruiting a diverse workforce. However, the work culture has not altered at the same rate that diverse personnel has grown. This has resulted in disproportionate and unrealistic bidding for BIPOC to assimilate (Blackburn, 2015; Hsu, 2017; Vinopal, 2016).

Diversity committees and task forces in academic libraries have been tasked with student outreach focused on matters surrounding diversity. Equally important, many of these groups have the responsibility of creating recruitment and retention opportunities for BIPOC library personnel, as well as diversity training for all library personnel. As previously discussed, the membership of these diversity committees or task forces are typically composed of several BIPOC, along with a few dedicated, active allies. Ergo, the task of retaining and influencing diversity at an organizational level becomes the burden of those who are in the minority the group is attempting to reach. This self-perpetuating cycle is unstainable.

Creating Equitable Division of Labor Surrounding DEI Topics

Alleviating Emotional Labor for BIPOC LIS Personnel

The obvious way of alleviating some of this diversity fatigue off the shoulders of BIPOC personnel is making sure that DEI work is evenly distributed throughout the organization. The importance of committees comes into play as it distributes efforts while having a specific outlet to deal with these issues within the institution. It shows that this needs to be a shared process both among BIPOC and non-BIPOC colleagues.

As often is the case, those that engage in DEI efforts (e.g., committees, policy adaptation) may be one of the few in an underrepresented group within their organization and they may feel the need to be a part of these initiatives. Early in their career BIPOC often feel they need to take on the emotional labor associated with DEI efforts, as doing so will ensure that their point of view will be heard and that any resulting guidance or policies will be more representative of their truth (Mathew et al., 2021). Furthermore, Jimenez et al. (2019) state that:

> Our survey findings indicate that traditionally marginalized groups are bearing the primary responsibility for creating a more diverse and inclusive culture ... Our results complement other studies that find underrepresented faculty are more likely to incorporate diversity-related content into course materials and contribute more to service than their peers.
>
> (p. 1031)

First, and foremost, it should be understood that DEI work should be everyone's responsibility in the organization. Part of knowing that everyone in the organization supports it is part of making the labor no more pressure than it needs to be as there will always be some kind of resistance from outside the organization. Furthermore, the upper administration needs to make it clear that they are behind all the efforts. A good example is the University of North Carolina at Chapel Hill starting the IDEA Action internal staff grant program, which has made grants available to all staff to fund the work of DEI. University Librarian Elaine L. Westbrooks states "... the only way to truly make change is to invest in it and support the people doing the work" (UNC Chapel Hill Libraries, 2021, para. 5).

Ways for LIS Professionals to Become Active Allies

The question always comes up of what more non-BIPOC can do to be an active ally for this work. The answer gets complex as being an ally can either help or add more labor to those it affects. Matthew et al. (2021) state that the term ally can be overseen as it being a continual process. Awareness of the issues is not enough, as being an active ally has more value to BIPOC causes. There is also the fact that ally voices should only be there to strengthen the cause, as voices in communities of color are strong and need to be respected as such (Chase, 2010).

Continuing education is key in helping on how allies should approach this work. BIPOC personnel will be more receptive to efforts knowing that there were efforts toward understanding the issues before just jumping into it. Even then, engaging in diversity education is an emotional labor in itself (Miller et al., 2019). At times, the simple acknowledgment and understanding that these efforts require more work helps with the settlement that traditionally this work is not recognized.

In addition, active allies need to understand that they will experience the same diversity fatigue that many BIPOC experience. Matthew et al. (2021) described White allies as having feelings of taxation, a need for sacrifice, and a paradox of words and actions. In summary, many allies may feel that they are ready to participate in the cause, but may not be ready for all that is meant to be a true ally. Though allies may know going into it that there will be a great deal of work involved, but may not be ready for all the mental side of it. Resistance to these diversity efforts can have both psychological and physical effects on those trying to support it (Thomas et al., 2020). This takes a great toll on those from underrepresented groups who have experienced it earlier in life and, therefore, comes as more of a shock to those who have not had any prior experience with this. Furthermore, people who may have not even experienced social justice events firsthand can still experience psychological distress (Ruggs et al., 2020).

Conclusion

Diversity fatigue in libraries is not solely a BIPOC problem; it negatively affects all library personnel. Diversity fatigue alters the emotional well-being of BIPOC library personnel. The heightened pressure—verbal, written, and suggested—placed on these particular employees to aid in the recruitment and retention of like personnel can lead to, "mental exhaustion" for BIPOC employees and may result in negative experiences, surrounding recruitment and retention for said employees or for the organization (Marie, 2013). Moreover, increased emphasis on performative DEI efforts, those not officially backed by library or campus policy, heightens the likelihood of diversity resistance and simultaneously decreases library personnel morale and efficiency (Farmanesh et al., 2020; Wasserman et al., 2008). Academic libraries must address the strife felt among their personnel, namely diversity resistance at all levels of the organization and diminished morale.

The emotional labor of DEI efforts can longer solely rest with BIPOC and active allies. Library administration must lead by example and encourage inactive majority culture library personnel to become active allies, so that diversity resistance is not stratified throughout the organization. A scaffolded model of diversity learning should be adapted, so that key concepts (e.g., cultural sensitivity, shared governance) become nested in the culture. Library personnel not already active in DEI efforts must hold space for the conversations, policies, and guidelines that are set forth by campus and library administration. It is in a shared accountability that the emotional labor that is often affiliated with DEI efforts may move beyond the diversity fatigue experienced by a minority population to that of a collective, equally divided experience.

Notes

1. This is akin to what occurs in corporations and nonprofit organizations.
2. Non-BIPOC persons may also be placed on said committees or task forces. However, research has shown that the psychological and labor-related consequences change based on ethnic and cultural background (Gorski, 2018).
3. A safe space is defined as a place where persons, especially those from marginalized communities may freely express themselves. In addition to one's home, college and university campuses are generally thought of as safe spaces. College or university libraries are deemed as a third safe space.

References

Blackburn, F. (2015, December 1). The intersection between cultural competence and whiteness in libraries. In the Library with the Lead Pipe. https://www.inthelibrarywiththeleadpipe.org/2015/culturalcompetence/

Blanche, A. (2018, April 4). *Diversity fatigue is real: Atlassian's state of diversity report 2018*. Medium. https://medium.com/smells-like-team-spirit/the-diversity-fatigue-is-real-atlassians-state-of-diversity-report-2018-2655d7eb5e2c

Chappell, B. (2021, June 25). *Derek Chauvin is sentenced to 22 1/2 years For George Floyd's Murder*. NPR. https://www.npr.org/sections/trial-over-killing-of-george-floyd/2021/06/25/1009524284/derek-chauvin-sentencing-george-floyd-murder.

Chase, S. E. (2010). *Learning to speak, learning to listen: How diversity works on campus*. Cornell University Press.

Dobbin, F., & Kalev, A. (2016). Why diversity programs fail. *Harvard Business Review, 94*(7/8), 52–60.

Farmanesh, P., Vehbi, A., Zargar, P., Sousan, A., & Bhatti, F. (2020). Is there always a positive relationship between workplace diversity and organizational performance, or does diversity fatigue imply a suppressing effect? *South East European Journal of Economics and Business, 15*(1), 14–26. https://doi.org/10.2478/jeb-2020-0002

Fernandez, J. P., & Davis, J. (1998). *Race, gender, and rhetoric: the true state of race and gender relations in corporate America*. McGraw-Hill.

Gorski, P. C. (2018). Racial battle fatigue and activist burnout in racial justice activists of color at predominantly white colleges and universities. *Race, Ethnicity, and Education, 22*(1)), 1–20. https://doi.org/10.1080/13613324.2018.1497966

Hartlep, N. D., & Ball, D. (2019). The battle of racial fatigue. In N. D. Hartlep & D. Ball (Eds.), *Racial battle fatigue in faculty* (pp. 1–13). Routledge Press. https://doi-org.proxy.lib.utk.edu/10.4324/9780429054013

Hsu, H. (2017, December 26). *The year in "diversity fatigue".* The New Yorker. https://www.newyorker.com/culture/2017-in-review/the-year-in-diversity-fatigue.

Jimenez, M. F., Laverty, T. M., Bombaci, S. P., Wilkins, K., Bennett, D. E., & Pejchar, L. (2019). Underrepresented faculty play a disproportionate role in advancing diversity and inclusion. *Nature Ecology & Evolution, 3*(7), 1030–1033. https://doi.org/10.1038/s41559-019-0911-5

Lam, M. B. (2018, September 23). *Diversity fatigue is real: And it afflicts the very people who are most committed to diversity work.* The Chronicle of Higher Education. https://www.chronicle.com/article/diversity-fatigue-is-real/.

Leon, R. A., & Williams, D. A. (2016). Contingencies for success: Diversity committees in higher education. *Innovative Higher Education, 41*(5), 395–410. https://doi.org/10.1007/s10755-016-9357-8

Mathew, A. C., Risdon, S. N., Ash, A., Cha, J., & Jun, A. (2021). The complexity of working with white racial allies: Challenges for diversity educators of color in higher education. *Journal of Diversity in Higher Education.* https://doi.org/10.1037/dhe0000310

Miller, R. A., Howell, C. D., & Struve, L. (2019). "Constantly, excessively, and all the time": The emotional labor of teaching diversity courses. *International Journal of Teaching and Learning in Higher Education, 31*(3), 491–502.

Miranda-Wolff, A. (2019). Experiential learning through cultural immersion. *Chief Learning Officer, 18*(1), 22–26, 64.

Nance-Nash, S. (2020, September 13). How corporate diversity initiatives trap workers of colour. *BBC.* https://www.bbc.com/worklife/article/20200826-how-corporate-diversity-initiatives-trap-workers-of-colour.

Ruggs, E. N., Summerville, K. M., & Marshburn, C. K. (2020). The response to social justice issues in organizations as a form of diversity resistance. In K. M. Thomas (Ed.), *Diversity resistance in organizations* (2nd ed., pp. 123–148). Routledge.

Smith, H. C. (2013). Diversity fatigue. *Network Journal, 20*(4), 60.

Thomas, K. M., & Plaut, V. C. (2008). The many faces of diversity resistance in the workplace. In K. M. Thomas (Ed.), *Diversity resistance in organizations* (pp. 1–22). Routledge.

Thomas, K. M., Lavner, J. A., Johnston, Z. E., & Scofield, C. (2020). Diversity performance, social surveillance and rescinding human rights: Understanding the health outcomes of diversity resistance. In K. M. Thomas (Ed.), *Diversity resistance in organizations* (2nd ed., pp. 1–20). Routledge.

UNC Chapel Hill Libraries. (2020, June 1). *The University Libraries' role in reckoning with systemic racism and oppression.* https://library.unc.edu/2020/06/the-university-libraries-role-in-reckoning-with-systemic-racism-and-oppression/.

UNC Chapel Hill Libraries. (2021, March 16). *Staff grants will advance equity and inclusion work at the university libraries.* https://library.unc.edu/2021/03/idea-action-grants/.

Vinopal, J. (2016, January 13). *The quest for diversity in library staffing: From awareness to action.* In the Library with the Lead Pipe. https://www.inthelibrarywiththeleadpipe.org/2016/quest-for-diversity/.

Wasserman, I. C., Gallegos, P. V., & Ferdman, B. M. (2008). Dancing with resistance. In K. M. Thomas (Ed.), *Diversity resistance in organizations* (pp. 175–200). Routledge.

Wexelbaum, R. S. (2017). *The library as safe space.* St. Cloud University. https://repository.stcloudstate.edu/cgi/viewcontent.cgi?referer=&httpsredir=1&article=1059&context=lrs_facpubs.

Index

CPSIA information can be obtained
at www.ICGtesting.com
Printed in the USA
BVHW020755240223
658750BV00034B/187